MENTAL MODELS

GENERAL THINKING CONCEPTS AND HOW TO USE ADVANCED
LEARNING STRATEGIES TO LEARN FAST ,TO IMPROVE
PRODUCTIVITY AT WORK AND IN RELATIONSHIP

By

Jack Collins

Contents

INTRODUCTION

Mental models help you understand life. For example, supply and demand is a mental model that helps you understand how the economy works. Game theory is a mental model that helps you understand how relationships and trust work. Entropy is a mental model that helps you understand how disorder and decay work.

Mental models also guide your perception and behavior. They are the thinking tools that you use to understand life, make decisions, and solve problems. Learning a new mental model gives you a new way to see the world—like Richard Feynman learning a new math technique.

Mental models are imperfect, but useful. There is no single mental model from physics or engineering, for example, that provides a flawless explanation of the entire universe, but the best mental models from those disciplines have allowed us to build bridges and roads, develop new technologies, and even travel to outer space. As historian Yuval Noah Harari puts it, "Scientists generally agree that no theory is 100 percent correct. Thus, the real test of knowledge is not truth, but utility."

The best mental models are the ideas with the most utility. They are broadly useful in daily life. Understanding these concepts will help you make wiser choices and take better actions. This is why developing a broad base of mental models is critical for anyone interested in thinking clearly, rationally, and effectively.

What is a Mental Model?

A mental model is an explanation of how something works. It is a concept, framework, or worldview that you carry around in your mind to help you interpret the world and understand the relationship between things. Mental models are deeply held beliefs about how the world works.

For example, supply and demand is a mental model that helps you understand how the economy works. Game theory is a mental model that helps you understand how relationships and trust work. Entropy is a mental model that helps you understand how disorder and decay work.

Mental models guide your perception and behavior. They are the thinking tools that you use to understand life, make decisions, and solve problems. Learning a new mental model gives you a new way to see the world—like Richard Feynman learning a new math technique.

Mental models are imperfect, but useful. There is no single mental model from physics or engineering, for example, that provides a flawless explanation of the entire universe, but the best mental models from those disciplines have allowed us to build bridges and roads, develop new technologies, and even travel to outer space. As historian Yuval Noah Harari puts it, "Scientists generally agree that no theory is 100 percent correct. Thus, the real test of knowledge is not truth, but utility."

The best mental models are the ideas with the most utility. They are broadly useful in daily life. Understanding these concepts will help you make wiser choices and take better actions. This is why developing a broad base of mental models is critical for anyone interested in thinking clearly, rationally, and effectively.

Mental model is the representation of a human mind's thought process. Everything that a person sees is been represented as models inside their minds. The mental models are considered as an internal scale for a human being for evaluation and for taking decisions. The Internal scales as mentioned by the scientists are ever changing and unstable as a human mind is susceptible to change due to adaptation. Even going through a change a human being must be able to evaluate and understand the consequences and results of change.

Mental model provide grounds for reasoning. The models that are made out of a person's perception and imagination which can influence reasoning than coming down to a logical conclusion. Out of all the possible assumptions, the mental model represents only the most relevant and true one. The contrary occurs when there is an alternative to reality.

Mental models have been utilized for studying human computer interaction (HCI), where the mental models are being utilized to make sense of the complexities that are around the people using computers. When people use computers, they build mental models in accordance with the interaction with the system. These models are used for interpreting the working of the system. For e.g.- People creates mental models before creating anything. It can be complicated machinery or even a simple apple pie. The creator thus creates a mental model which he refers to while materializing it.

Scope

The concept of mental model can be applied to a variety of fields such as psychology, business, technology, Human Nature & Judgment etc. People utilize these mental models to make sense of the reality. The practical and the theoretical knowledge each gained is applied in these models to further understand and to refer about the world they are living. Inventors comprehend the mental model of the consumers to understand their demands and needs. And in business, People use mental models to do daily purchase more economically.

Developing Your Self Concept

Self concept encompasses beliefs, perceptions and expectations as the core of your self-identity. Although it differs from self-esteem, it does influence your feelings of self-worth and the way you perceive your relationship to the world. The development of the characteristic is greatly influenced by other people in your life, so living in accordance with your beliefs requires that you take the time to truly know yourself.

Development

A child's self identity generally focuses on simple characteristics, such as hair color and collection of toys, while an adult's self-identity includes abstract and multifaceted ideas. We grow through the actions we take through various experiences and through the ideas we form from them.

As you look back on your past experiences and the choices you've made throughout your life, you will probably see some conflict between your own thoughts on the matters and the opinions you heard from others. How did these conflicts and experiences shape the expectations you have for yourself and others? Do these expectations match your belief system? How well do you identify with the beliefs and actions of those around you? Self-concept determines whether a person feels he belongs in certain social groups, and a clash of beliefs with expectations can create emotional or social turmoil.

Components

This concept is abstract and covers all areas of a person's role in the world. Your physical appearance is one component of your identity, which can influence your self-esteem and determine the social groups you feel you belong to. Are you an insider? An outsider? As you join groups or identify with others, your mind forms the social component that influences your thoughts and behaviors. It is your academic achievement, though, that forms many of your personal expectations. The academic component is not necessarily focused on your grades-it's more of a sense of identity that comes from your areas of interest or expertise. Do you excel in the arts? In math?

The beliefs you form through experience and through interactions with others will also influence your relationship to the many mysteries in life. Do you believe in the supernatural? Do you rely on science for explanations?

Conflicts within Concept

A healthy sense of self and level of self-esteem can improve all areas of your life, as it establishes your code of conduct within relationships and increases your motivation to reach for personal goals. Taking the time to reflect on your experiences and to truly know yourself can help you settle conflict between your personal beliefs and what you hear or perceive from others in your life. Ask yourself if your personal identity stems from your inner workings or from what you've been told by others. Remember, though, that the middle ground is quite often the most realistic.

Improvement

The difference between improvement of self-esteem and improvement of your own concept of yourself is that the former is an effect brought about by action taken on the latter. When you doubt your ability to do something, positive affirmations or self-talk can help you find the courage to try; but it's the concrete accomplishment that shapes your true perception of self. Start small, but challenge yourself! Make time to try things that interest you, and take the time to think about its overall effect on your life.

Listen to the positive inner voice and aim to live in a manner that reflects your true beliefs. As you challenge your own ideas and learn from new experiences, you may find that some of your beliefs have changed or that you've inadvertently improved your social relationships. A combination of self concept reflection and self-esteem improvement strategies can help you reach seemingly unattainable goals!

Develop Your Self Esteem

What is Self Esteem?

Self-esteem is the combination of: self-worth, self-regard, self-respect, and self-integrity. It is a psychological concept used to describe how an individual feels about him/herself. High self-esteem indicates a high worth placed on the self while low self-esteem indicates the opposite.

Abraham Maslow believes that psychological health is based on the core, and it is only possible whenever the essential core of the person is fundamentally accepted, loved and respected by others and by her or his self. According to Jack Canfield: "*Self-esteem is based on feeling capable and feeling lovable*".

Self-esteem and self-image are interrelated. The term self-image is used to describe a person's mental picture of himself. Self-image leads to self-esteem. During early childhood, we develop mental images of ourselves: who we are, what we are good at, how we look, and what are our strengths and weakness could be. Our experiences and our interactions with other people will make these mental images stronger inside us. Over time these mental self-images will develop our notion of self-esteem. Self-esteem is about feelings that we develop inside ourselves as a result of outside factors. Self-esteem is about how much we feel accepted, loved and valued by others and how much we accept, love and value ourselves. It is the combination of those two factors that shape our self-esteem.

Typically, self-esteem is defined in terms of how we evaluate ourselves and our characteristics. According to Stanley Coppersmith, a pioneering researcher in the field, it is "personal judgment of worthiness that is expressed in the attitudes the individual holds toward himself."

Good self-esteem means that we have enough self-confidence to not need the approval of others.

How it is Developed?

Thoughts, relationships and experiences create your self-esteem. Self-esteem begins to form as early as childhood, and factors that influence it include the likes of one's own thoughts and perceptions, how other people react, experiences at school, work and the community, disability, illness, injury, culture, religion, and even one's role and status in society. Low self-esteem is developed when the person doesn't see himself as having the qualities he admires. Unfortunately, persons with low self-esteem usually do have the qualities they admire but they can't see it because they programmed their self-image that way. Dr. Michael Miller, editor in chief of the Harvard Mental Health Letter, says, "It's more likely that self-esteem will come as a result of accurate self-understanding, appreciation of one's genuine skills, and the satisfaction of helping others." People close to you like: parents, siblings, peers, friends, teachers and other contacts and your interaction with those people, will have a big impact on your self-esteem. Self-esteem is established in your early childhood, and it matures during late adolescence. Whenever the person stabilizes their sense of being in control of their own destiny, they begin to formulate self-esteem. Family relationship plays a major role in determining our self-esteem. It is how we are treated by others that teach us whether we are important. The feeling of being cared for or worthwhile will shape our level of self-esteem. This is linked to receiving approval from others. Yet based on early life experiences and their social roles, women often seek approval more than men. By age 16, more girls than boys begin to report low self-esteem. According to Dove Research: The Real Truth about Beauty: 7 in 10 girls believe they are not good enough or do not measure up in some way including their looks, performance in school and relationships.

How Important is Self Esteem?

According to Brian Tracy: *"Your self-esteem is probably the most important part of your personality. It precedes and predicts your performance in almost everything you do. Your level of self-esteem is really your level of mental fitness. To perform at your best and to feel terrific about yourself, you should be in a perpetual state of self-esteem."*

Self-esteem is important for people as it gives them more confidence to face life. Self-esteem will enable the person to have more optimism and have more momentum to reach their goals. Persons with low self-esteem usually feel inferior and may not perform well under different circumstances. They developed false thoughts that no one will accept them or like them. On the other hand, people with healthy self-esteem can feel good about their environment and then about themselves. They can do things more efficiently and by doing so; they can feel proud of their accomplishments and about themselves.

Feeling good bout ourselves will enable us to enjoy life more and more. Feeling that we are accepted, liked and loved, means we have healthy self-esteem, and this feeling will be reflected in our relationships.

One of the major causes of broken relationships is low self-esteem.

Developing self-esteem enables us to invite happiness in our lives. It is this feeling that makes you believe that you deserve happiness. It is very important to understand this belief, the belief that you really deserve to be happy and fulfilled, because with this belief you can treat people with respect, and goodwill, thus favoring rich interpersonal relationships and avoiding destructive ones. Possessing little self-regard can lead people to become depressed, to fall short of their potential, or to tolerate abusive situations and relationships. Many studies show that low self-esteem leads to stress, depression and anxiety. Research indicates a positive relationship between healthy self-esteem and many positive results, including happiness, humility, resilience and optimism. Self-esteem plays a role in almost everything you do.

World Health Organization recommends in "Preventing Suicide" published in 2000, that strengthening students' self-esteem is important to protect children and adolescents against mental distress and despondency, enabling them to cope adequately with difficult and stressful life situations. In the book: Alcoholism: A False Stigma: Low Self-Esteem the True Disease, (1996) Candito reports: "Those who have identified themselves as "recovered alcoholics" indicate that low self esteem is the most significant problem in their lives. Low self-esteem is the true problem and the true disease. Alcohol is but a symptom of an alcoholic's disease". According to Glenn R. Schiraldi, who is Ph.D., author of The Self-Esteem Workbook and a professor at the University Of Maryland School Of Public Health:"Those with good self-esteem are able to realistically and honestly evaluate their strengths, weaknesses and potential." According to Madelyn Swift, our emotional health depends on our self esteem. Liking ourselves and feeling capable are the foundations on which emotional health rests.

Power Tips to Jumpstart Your Self-Esteem

Self-esteem is the ideas, values, and beliefs that you hold about yourself and how you feel that you are viewed and perceived by the world. Your self-esteem feeds your self-concept, which in turn fuels your mental health and overall sense of well-being.

According to Nathaniel Branden: "If you feel inadequate to face challenges, feel unworthy of love and respect, un-entitled to happiness, fear assertive thoughts wants and needs; if you lack basic self-trust, self-respect and self-confidence, your self-esteem deficiency will limit you no matter what other assets you possess."

People with healthy self-esteem strive to reach their full potential; they see themselves as being competent, confident and capable of achieving their goals and desires.

If your self-esteem is in need of a boost, look no further - here are 7 powerful tips that will jump-start your self-esteem.

Control The Inner Critic

Try to stop thinking negative thoughts about you. Let go of your shortcomings, start thinking about the positive qualities that you possess. Counter your negative thinking by saying something positive about yourself. Each day, write down three things about yourself that you are proud of.

Set Goals

List at least three things that you would love to have the courage to do. Then formulate a plan to actually do them. Set yourself up for success by breaking big goals into daily action steps and take time to acknowledge and celebrate the small successes. This will feed your need for recognition and provides the extra push to keep you moving forward. Rewards could be as simple as giving your self permission to enjoy hat delectable piece of cheesecake you saw in the bakery or as huge as giving yourself a dream vacation. Either way, it is important for you to celebrate your successes.

Develop Your Silly Bone

Become a Master of Silliness a Guru of Play. Bring more laughter and fun into your life. Make a list of what you love to do, starting from childhood until now, and try to find time to do it at least once a week, even if it's just for a few minutes.

Enjoy spending time with the people you care about and doing the things you love. Relax and have a good time - and avoid putting your life on hold.

Reframe Your View of Mistakes

Give yourself a break and accept that you will make mistakes. View your mistakes as learning opportunities that make people interesting. Mistakes provide you with important information - you now know what doesn't work. Think of Thomas Edison and the invention of the light bulb; how many mistakes did he make before finally succeeding?

Get out of Your Own Head

Know when you are looping and circulating thoughts in your own head. Find and list ways that you can use to shift and change your physiology quickly. Exercise, connect with nature, listen to music, etc. Stop thinking about you. This may sound strange, but low self-esteem is often accompanied by too much focus on the self. Doing something that absorbs you and holds your attention can quickly get you out of yourself and help you to feel better.

Clear out the junk: This means anything hurtful and unconstructive that you've been told by someone you care for, cared about, (or even someone you didn't) is to be taken with a grain of salt. It is one thing to be given constructive feedback in life, but quite another when people are downright mean and unkind. Remember it's the offending party's issue, NOT yours. Take what applies when receiving feedback and leave the rest

The single most important power technique that you can take to improve the quality of your life is that of gratitude.

Being grateful and counting your blessings for the simplest things can be the most empowering thing that you can do for your mental health. You begin to notice your strengths, you begin to see what you have, you begin to appreciate the simple things in life, including being grateful for the things people actually take for granted, such as food and shelter, access to a computer, etc.

Know and Operate from Your Own Personal Values:

Realize once and for all that your self-worth and self-esteem is defined by you and only you. You cannot rely on someone else for your happiness. Another person's view of you is immaterial. Happiness and self-esteem comes from inside of you!

Think Creatively

Creative individuals, truly, are 'unreasonable' because they defy the norm, and are undaunted by the grotesque and the abnormal. They delight in dallying amorously with the unusual, the unorthodox and the unconventional. Every progress and every advance that humanity has so far attained is due to the creative powers of exceptional minds.

One may master all the rules of rational thinking and the principles of logic: it will not help. The pursuit of knowledge, the discovery of truth, and the wisdom of life, in truth, fall incalculably outside the ordered realm of rationalism and logic; for life is too fluent and too changeful interspersed with shocks and surprises. The puzzles of life cannot always be cracked with stereotyped responses; they call for creative examination.

Creativeness calls for the courage to conceive ideas and visualise events outside the orbit of logic and the realm of rationality. In popular language, it is known as 'thinking outside the box'! That is what creativity is all about: taking the un-trodden path that no one has taken before! Creativeness is the unfettering of intellectual imprisonment from the shackles of conventional and conservative dogmatism.

Impossible it will be for any individual to be creative who locks himself in the chambers of dogmatic intellectualism and contents himself in the narrow boundaries of axiomatic theories. Creative thinkers share certain characteristics in common: they do not fear stepping into unfamiliar domains; they unflappably flirt with unrelated fields of knowledge; and they enthusiastically undertake voyages into unknown disciplines. If truth be uttered, creativity is not for those who are impoverished in the quest for imaginative thinking.

Most of us are held back in our assumption that creativity is always about discovering or inventing something fundamentally new or novel, and therefore, it is a prerogative of a gifted few. What an unalloyed misconception!

For a fact, creativity is an aptitude to relate seemingly unrelated concepts into something exceptionally different. Creativity flowers through the convergence of disparate ideas, concepts or thoughts.

Linear Thinking Versus Intersectional Thinking

Since formal education is designed to master the fundamentals of specialist disciplines, it, dutifully, shapes the mind in the mould of linearity. In other words, linearity is one-dimensional thinking! It subjects the mind to inquire in terms of reasoning and logical analysis whilst depriving, at the same time, the ability to think outside the beaten track. It, thus, becomes an exercise in mastering the mundane and the monotonous making predictable changes along the way.

Linear thinking is incapable of stirring radical changes because it limits the expanse of its circle within which it conducts its adventure in learning. It dares not step out of the circle as it satiates itself with making little improvements here and minor changes there with minimal disruption to the status quo. Most of the innovations stimulated by linear thinking are of this kind: policy changes, process changes, structural changes fall into the linear category. These are not earth-shattering or life-changing transformations but incremental improvements.

Intersectional thinking, in contrast, moves in unpredictable directions, which, as a consequence, can change the context radically.

Intersectional thinking uninhibitedly cuts through various fields, disciplines, areas and domains to create connections between seemingly unrelated ideas and concepts; it creates breakthrough ideas and concepts.

Examples in intersectional thinking abound: whether it is Steve Jobs integrating the aesthetics that he learned through the course in calligraphy and integrating that knowledge into iMacs, iPods, iPhones or iPads; whether it is Alexander Graham Bell who had combined his interests in mechanics, ventriloquism, speech therapy and music to invent the telephone; or whether it is Leonardo da Vinci who drew his abundance of knowledge and inspiration from the various disciplines such as engineering, sculpting, painting, architecture, geology and anatomy-they all point to the ability of these men to relate the unrelated into a unique outcome.

As a rule, intersectional thinking demands an open mind to connect concepts and theories from one discipline with concepts and theories in another. Whether it is about food recipe, telecom networks or academic research, linking unrelated concepts is a thing of beauty in itself and it lies at the core of creativity. Intersectional thinking is easy since its secret lies in the interlinking and interlocking of disparate ideas and bringing about a synthesis.

Barriers To Creative Thinking

Creativity cannot be bought or faked; nor can it be learned from books but it can be developed with a little adjustment in how we think. The barriers to creativity reside in the mind as conceptual blocks freezing our ability to conceive alternative solutions and ideas to problems and constraints. At every moment, each one of us is bombarded with far more countless sensations than we can possibly handle. As you read this, you probably are not aware of the existence of your eyes, the sounds in the background or the feel of your clothes on your skin. Even though all of this information is available, you probably were not aware of any of it until and unless you consciously paid attention to those sensations.

We obviously cannot pay attention to the infinite stream of stimuli competing with one another to grab our conscious attention. Doing so would subject us to information overload and drive us to madness. Hence, we filter out those stimuli that are not relevant and selectively attend to those that we deem useful for our purpose. This selective attention, aside its usefulness, censors vital and useful clues which probably could have life-changing potential.

Formal education has moulded us to think in terms of logic and reason. The obsession with 'right' answers has always taken precedence over 'imagination' whilst at work. The fetishism with the proper way to do things has been given importance over 'innovativeness'. This has led to the petering out of improvisation and experimentation killing creativity in the process.

Creativity often suffers at the hands of four shortcomings: constancy, commitment, compression and complacency.

Constancy: A universal principle has been decreed upon us that constancy in thought, word and deed is a virtue. Any individual lacking in constancy is liable to be labelled as untrustworthy, unreliable and undesirable. In organisations, the primary function of control systems is to minimise deviation from the established standard. Constancy, doubtless, is taken to a divine status in the everyday scheme of things.

Yet, upon closer scrutiny, the same constancy, that aims to bring expected results, stamps underfoot the speck of creativity struggling to unleash its creative expression.

Most people, when confronting a problem, deal with it based on their past experiences or look for a precedence in resolving it. They think vertically! Not laterally! A vertical focus assumes a narrow gaze defining the problem in only one way rather than interpreting it in multiple ways. Any individual possessed by a conviction that it is not worth considering many alternatives will remain incapacitated in creative thinking.

The bane of constancy also arises in limiting oneself to subjecting a problem to single interpretation. A problem, for instance, can be defined and assessed in multiple interpretations: through non-verbal or symbolic interpretation, numerically or algebraically; using sensory impressions such as smell, taste, sound, touch, seeing; through feelings and emotions such as excitement, happiness, anger, hatred; or using visual imagery such as mental maps. The more variegated the interpretation of a problem, the better are the chances of coming up with creative outcomes.

Constancy is inimical to creativity. Constancy is nothing but a procession of sameness, or similarity

Commitment: Another virtue that stands as an obstacle to creativity is commitment. It causes the creative juices to freeze especially when we define problems in the light of past experiences. The general human tendency is to see current problems as variations of past occurrences, hence we develop solutions similar to the ones that have worked in the past, totally oblivious that problems can be seen in new ways and interpreted differently. The commitment to the past enables us to deal with problems only stereotypically, not innovatively.

Commitment to a particular viewpoint may also inhibit in seeing commonalities among different problems and coming up a single idea that addresses many issues at the same time. Viewing disparate elements holistically is an attribute of creative thinkers. Ray Kroc, the man behind the creation of McDonald's did not invent fast food. He was a salesman before he connected different ideas into something unique. Connecting a standardised menu, uniform cooking methods, consistent service quality, hygiene in facilities, low cost food production and disposable eating materials, whilst combining them with his sales experience, negotiating talent, relationship building, entrepreneurial ambition, he demonstrated a unique approach to creativity. Not one individual attribute mentioned above is unique but he integrated them to produce an idea that, to this day, remains a powerful and profitable business model.

Compression: Too much information and too much data are adequate to drive anyone crazy. In addition, time pressure and resource scarcity constrain our ability to look at a problem widely. In the process, we screen out a lot of details. We impose artificial constraints upon ourselves when we deal with problems. We draw boundaries, sit inside them and conjure up answers to our riddles. There is an aversion either due to personal choice or impersonal influences to brainstorm adequately in dealing with problems. Often, people make assumptions without recognising them and exploring available alternatives to tap into hidden clues.

Compression also saps the ability to sift the wheat from the chaff-an ability to cull out inaccurate, misleading or irrelevant information. Indiscriminate minds weave a mishmash of data into a chaotic bundle only to become burdened by its weight. It increases complexity of the problem whilst defying the simplicity of problem definition.

Complacency: Simply interpreted, it is mental laziness! It arises out of lack of curiosity and aversion to mental work. Unwillingness to ask questions, procrastination to learn and fear of embarrassment of exposing one's ignorance are some of the reasons why people become less curious. Two aspects are vital here: 1) an enthusiasm to ask questions and 2) an eagerness to find answers.

Overcome mental inertia! Creativity happens when you use the right side of your brain which is concerned with intuition, synthesising and playfulness. Our highly structured education and regimented work tend to lay emphasis on using more of the left part of the brain which is responsible for logical, analytical and sequential tasks, and rarely its counterpart sitting at the opposite end.

Use both sides of the brain to be creative. Whilst the right hemisphere helps in germinating creative ideas, its left counterpart complements by processing and interpreting them through logical analysis.

How to Simplify Thinking and Everything

We all face the difficulties in life, especially when we must think instead of simply accepting. We all ask: Can we simplify our life? Can we find one simple concept that is sufficient for analyzing, managing, and innovating anything and everything? Can we solve any problem or win any competition using one simple concept? Have you ever wondered if we could reduce everything to one concept?

Here are some Idea worth knowing.

For any business of life, my point of view is that, every activity is based on some common points. If we can understand those common points present in any activity, we can definitely avoid mistakes and make success certain. But what is meant by these common points

In anything, person, group, time, space or activity whatever is similar, repeating, between or that is common is the common point. Anything that is common over time or across space is common point. Anything common among in personal efforts or in collective initiatives is common point. Thus in any activity in all walks of life or in any maneuver the thing which plays the central role is the common point in that activity.

For better understanding we can say that whatever creates a relation among things by connecting them, establishes a contact between them, as a result of which some activity comes into existence is the common point.

For example, in any business entity, the personality of the leader of the organization is the common point. The leader through the charm of his personality, and abilities and competencies not only binds the team together but also motivates the team to work harder as a result of which the organization progresses and the business earn higher profit. Contrary to this, if the personality of the leader is weak, regardless of the best of plans and high skill of labor, the results will be opposite.

People compete for things which they consider to have value. There is a common point, or agreement that something is of value worth expenditure. Contrary to this, people cooperate when faced with mutual threat. This mutual threat is a common point.

Like there are nerves in body which connect each part of body with brain, they take signals from body to brain and commands from brain to body, and act as common point between body and brain, there are common points in any system, organization or setup. Through the knowledge of these points, we can analyze, manage or innovate the existing setup. The most important systems in our life is our mind.

In any sphere of life, our decisions shape our life. These decisions are based on our thinking, and our analysis of situation. Thus, it is our thinking that shapes our life. In this view, the most important activity in our life is thinking. Thinking for analyzing situations, and for innovating new outcomes. If we can demonstrate the importance of common points, demonstrate that they play central role in the thinking, we can also demonstrate their importance in every struggle of life.

Let us observe something we all went through in last few minutes.

As you are reading this, your mind is processing this information. Did it happen that while listening to this, you heard of some word, phrase or sentence, and it reminded you of something else? It happened. Did it not? Although you were listening to this lecture, a part of this lecture made you recall something different, perhaps irrelevant.

It happens a lot. Every time you listen, read, observe one thing, another idea pops up in your mind, and the reason it comes is that your mind picks a part of what you are consciously observing and forms a bridge between your conscious observation and something else in mind.

Let us go through another example to clarify this. Let us say, your friend remarks about the freshness of fruits when you both are in market. This idea of 'fresh' helps you recall that another friend asked you to buy a fresh cake for party. But the 'cake' is sweet, so you recall. And eating 'sweet' can cause problems for your 'diabetes' and for keeping your 'diabetes' in check, you should regularly take 'medicine'. But, you recall that your 'medicine' are about to end and you should 'buy more medicine'. For 'buying more medicine', you decide to drive to nearest medical store after buying the fruits in this market.

This journey of thoughts from freshness of fruits to deciding to drive to medical store was possible through a series of points that formed a bridge.

Each time, you come across an idea, a component of the idea helps you recall another idea. In above examples, they are 'fresh', 'cake', 'sweet', 'diabetes', 'take medicine', and 'buy medicine'. These ideas form a bridge between current thought and immediate next idea. Individually they are common points between two consecutive ideas and collectively they are common point between two remote ideas of 'freshness' and 'driving'.

This is how we move from one idea to another. This is fluidity of imagination. It is also a very powerful method of creative thinking.

In this example we were recalling things, but we can also confuse things, merge them, and create new ones in the same fashion. For example, think of yourself making a cup of tea. You add hot water, a tea bag and sugar in a cup. From 'hot water' you recall drinking 'lemon' with warm water yesterday, for the first time which was a great experience. Coming back to tea, you decide to add some lemon in this mixture of warm water with tea. You end up creating a new tea for yourself. It is black tea with lemon. The common point 'hot water' helped you connect two ideas of black tea and lemon which were initially separate.

Definitely, it is the same way someone innovated mobile phones with camera by observing the common trait that both can be held in hand. This hand held feature was the common point. Perhaps, he observed this feature by chance or due to the desire to take and send a photo to a loved one through phone. However, this common point enabled him to combine the two machines.

Had cameras being big like cars, or had the common point between camera and mobile remained unobserved, you would never take selfies. How sad would that be? So once you take selfie, never forget common points and their power to innovate, and invent.

But is the application of common points only limited to memory recall, and innovation? No. It extends to logic, critical thinking and analysis of observation.

Like the fluidity, and memory recall, our concepts are overlapping and mixed. Some ideas which are part of broader ideas, can form a bridge between two broader ideas. In some cases, they can form bridge between opposing ideas and help us to turn the argument against its proponent.

For example, someone argues that 'everyone has freedom to do whatever he or she wishes. Therefore, there must not be any restrictions at all'. From this argument it follows that one is not restricted from suppressing freedom of others. Thus, as a result, the chances are that there will be at least one individual who will not have freedom to do at least one thing he or she wishes. This contradicts the claim that everyone has freedom to do whatever he or she wishes.

As we can see, the idea that 'one is not restricted from suppressing freedom of others' follows from the conclusion of argument 'there must not be any restrictions at all' and connects it with the opposite of premise of argument 'Everyone has freedom to do whatever he or she wishes'. As a result, it is common between two opposite ideas.

This is why some philosopher once remarked: Every thesis has seeds of its own negation. Thus any argument may be turned on its head, by identifying something within the premises of the argument and using it to produce a conclusion that contradicts initial argument.

But the role of common points extends beyond simple negation. They in fact create arguments, and enable conclusions. For example, I say: Tech companies are hiring AI experts these days. All AI experts are experts of formal thinking. Therefore, tech companies are hiring experts of formal thinking. By being common between two ideas of Tech companies hiring and expert of formal thinking, the terms 'AI expert' enables us to conclude something about the relation of these two ideas.

However, due to their conclusive power, the common points can be deceptive. Consider another argument: Knowledge is power. Power tends to corrupt. Therefore, knowledge corrupts.

Here apparently the term 'power' is common point but it has been used in two different meanings. The power that corrupts is power over humans and power that comes from knowledge is power over one's own weaknesses. Therefore, it is not a common between the two ideas.

Unwary of this dual meaning, reader can be deceived into believing knowledge is corrupt. This technique of argumentation is employed by fanatic leaders, mostly religious.

Thus, for clear thinking, which we must do for shaping our lives better, we must identify and refine our understanding of common points in any argument. For analyzing any argument, we must focus on the common points in it, we must identify their presence and absence, their definitions and uses.

Just like there can be the same concept common between two concepts which enables inference, sometime we can identify similarities common between two things to conclude something. This is called analogies. For example, this presentation is getting long like river Nile. This length is the common trait between the two - my presentation and Nile. Thus, due to similarity it can be concluded that I will talk even more. However, a good presentation should be like a woman's skirt; long enough to cover the subject and short enough to create interest. Thus, we can conclude that I will finish it soon. But we will see which inference is correct, and which analogy worked in.

In analogies too, common points of similarities enable us to conclude and therefore these can be deceptive too. We must then be careful when establishing similarities.

Not only similarities between two things but a pattern that is common across several things helps us classify things or make abstractions. For example, we observe that the animals that breast feed give birth rather than lay eggs. Thus we generalize that all animals that breast feed give birth. Although, a breast feeding animal may lay egg. For example, Duck-billed platypus. Thus, again common points or common traits enable us to generalize, but caution is needed.

Similarly, if a pattern is common over time it can be useful for forecasting or may indicate relation of cause and effect. For example, every time the central bank announces something financial market shows increased volatility. One may suggest that the announcements are cause of increased volatility. However, such generalizations are suggestive only, and hardly conclusive.

This way our entire thinking, our very foundation of life, because our thinking shapes our life, simply works because of ideas that form a bridge, ideas that are same, similar, or are repeating. These are common between other ideas. Therefore, these are common points. It is these common points that allow us to recall, innovate, classify, deduce or infer.

In short think of a chain tied to a stone. Each link of chain ensures that the whole chain acts as one unit and enables you to pull the stone in desired direction. However, if even one link in chain breaks, you will not be able to pull the stone. Just like these links of chain, our thoughts, actions, relations, systems or anything depends on those points that enable connection between two or more points. These links are common points. And just like each link of chain connects with an immediate next link, common points connect with immediate next one only. A lack of common point between two points mean that they cannot work together like a system.

Our thinking is governed by common points. But, we can consciously analyze them for avoiding any mistakes, and for determinedly managing and deliberately innovating new outcomes. Just like we breathe naturally, but we can deliberately alter rhythm of breathing to achieve certain psychological state, we can deliberately use the common points, which already use naturally, to achieve our goals.

By consciously observing the common points, refining them, managing them and innovating them we can analyze, manage and innovate anything and everything. We simplify. We reduce every situation to one idea. The idea of common points. That is whatever is same, similar, repeating and is in between two or more things, actions, time or ideas.

As the common points play central role in our thinking, and our thinking shapes our life, it is necessary to analyze the common points in every sphere of life too. Thus for problem solving we must refine our understanding of the common points.

Now the question we need to answer is simply one question: What are common points in our present problem situation?

For answering this one question, we need to focus on four concepts. We will go through these four concept now, before describing seven steps needed to implement the system for analyzing, managing, or innovating through common points.

First of all, we observe things that are common across time or individuals because they are repeating, either over time, or across individuals. For example, you wish to advertise your product. And you observe that every time there is a football match, most of people gather around television, even those who would not watch usually. Therefore, you can use this repetition over time, which is predictable, for promoting your product to most people.

Likewise, you may observe a repeating pattern among young people in an area. You find out their desire to learn music. If you know music, you have found a possible way, either to network with them, or to sell them some lessons.

Now another thing is to find anyone or anything that is common between two or more others. For example, the intermediaries such as wholesalers of product market exist between the producers and buyers. They connect the two which is positive function. However, they hoard to increase the prices which is negative function. A government regulation, increased tax or subsidy, which influence these intermediaries will influence both buyers and producers indirectly because the intermediaries will adjust their behavior accordingly.

Next you may now observe things that are same. For example, you may find out that the same person who is your neighbor is also member of a research organization that you wish to join. You can ask him to guide you and perhaps assist you to become a member. This person is, therefore, common between you and the organization you wish to join.

Like same, another concept is similar. Similarities allow for analogies which are a powerful means for either communicating ideas or feeling to those who have not experienced them, or for understanding aspects of a thing similar to another.

An example of analogies is poetry. Faiz, a poet from Asia, is known for his use of analogies. He wrote a poem for his beloved, expressing how he missed her. He said, in the desert of my solitude, my love, quiver the shadows of your voice, the mirage of your lips. By using the analogies of desert, quivering, and mirage he expressed how he missed his beloved in a way that now anyone who understand the common point of desert, quiver and mirage can grasp the intensity of his desire to unite with his beloved.

Analogies help us express our ideas to those who have not learnt them by using ideas that are commonly understood by all of us and have similarities with our ideas which we wish to express. Thus, in communication using analogies there are two common points. One is that ideas used as analogies are commonly understood by all, and two these ideas used as analogies and the idea which we wish to communicate using these analogies have common traits or common points.

Now the question you must ask is: How can we use this idea of common points for analyzing, managing and innovating?

To analyze, manage and innovate using the common points, we must identify, refine, modify and remove them. To do so, we must ask a series of questions. These questions should help us identify and refine them, before we can modify, remove or add new points. The goal is to see entire situation as a set of common points knit together along with other points, and through the understanding of nature of these points, we should be able to see the map of all possibilities, possibilities of change. There is a seven step process as follow:

Step 1: Identify:

What are the common points?

That which is same, similar, between or repeating in time periods, things, spaces, people, ideas and actions etc.

Step 2: Challenge:

Are we perceiving a common point which in fact does not exist?

Challenge your observation by asking: Is that really so? What if it is not?

Are there some common points which we are unaware of?

Step 3: Refine:

Is there any ambiguity or vagueness in understanding of the common points?

Recall the example of knowledge is power. The word 'power' was ambiguous. Each common point must have a clear definition. There must not be any overlapping, fuzzy, unclear meanings.

Do we lack some information about a common points?

It is possible that some common points are hidden deep within apparent observations. You need to dig deep within.

Do we confuse two or more common points to be one or overlapping?

For example, etiquettes of meeting are common point between people of a culture. Etiquettes for meeting close friends are not same as those for strangers. One may confuse the two etiquettes assuming that after all both strangers and friends are humans.

Are the common points found immediate to the points between which they are common?

For example, let us observe a, b, c, d, and e, and the c is exactly in middle of a, and e but not the common between a, and e. In this case, b, c, and d are collectively common between and a, and e while b is common between a, and c just like c is common between b and d and d between c and e.

The aim should be to knit the whole picture without any missing piece of information, without any jump, and to move from one point to only immediate next one. So that we can see all the possibilities. Recall, the earlier example of going to market of fresh fruits and deciding to drive to buy medicine. A jump from fresh fruits to driving would not justify why and how we suddenly decided to go to medicine when we are simply buying fresh fruits.

Step 4: Explain:

What is the nature of the common points?

Their definitions, functions, limitations, and reasons of existence.

Step 5: Knit the picture:

What are the other points between which they are common?

How do they relate to other points between which they are common?

Step 6: Innovate and manage:

How can each of them be modified?

For example, a common wall exists between my office room and my library. I wish to have a quick access to next room. I can modify the wall and make a doorway.

How can there be a deliberate introduction of a new common point?

For example, there is no intercom between my room and another room where my father works. I can add an intercom which will be a common point for quick communication.

How can some common point be avoided? Or can some of them be deleted from the system?

For example, one of the windows of my room opens towards a school. During mid-day break, the kids come to play ground and play. This creates much noise. And the window acts as a common point for allowing this to come to my room. The glass panes of window were not sound proof. What I did was to buy new glass panes which were sound proof and close my windows during the midday break. This way, I avoid the common point which allows for the noise to come in my room when I need to.

Step 7: The big picture:

What is the picture of the entire situation with our knowledge of common points?

With this basic setup you can identify, analyze, manage, and innovate any situation, or solve problem. You have learned how the common points can be used to create and analyze arguments, and how these points can be used to innovate, and manage anything in life. This basic setup equips you with everything you need for simplifying your life. However, necessary knowledge is not sufficient for practical affairs of life. The application of this to specific areas of life is needed.

Just like the mind is the most important system in our lives, and it is a common point in every activity of our lives, economic activity influences our lives too. Everyone engages in an economic activity, be it not for profit organization, labor supply, own business or investing. The economic activity has an influence on rest of activities of our lives. Therefore, economic activity is another common point in our lives. Because it is central, it is between other actions, it repeatedly influences our life. In economic activity, the central role is of competition. Whether it is NGO, or any business people compete each other for there is an agreement. The agreement that the money is important for living, the money is central for our modern lives as we no longer live in primitive communal tribes. Thus, competition is a common point because it is central in economic activity, it is between all activities in market, it repeatedly influences all decisions, and is same in all forms of activities. This means that one of the important common point in life is competition.

Everyone faces competition in life. In life either we fight or we run forever. If we run, we end up exhausted, and unfulfilled. Thus, our only option is to fight, to struggle and to compete. But if we are not equipped with tools and knowledge of competition, we inevitably loose our precious time, and scarce resources. We lose competitions too. Thus, there is a need to learn competition.

ADVANCED LEARNING STRATEGIES

Everybody wants to pick up new skills fast. For example, most people would want to learn how to make money fast or pick up any girl fast. So how do you learn fast to pick up skills faster?

Well the best way to learn fast is to fail fast. That's in my opinion is how you learn fast.

What do I mean when I say to fail fast? I mean that you should just pick up the skills you want to develop and just do it. And when you don't succeed at the skill, you 'try' again. That's how you fail fast. To fail slow is when you do a skill and you don't succeed, you think about your failure and you stop yourself trying to do the skill again or you leave it later.

For instance, you are doing a math test and you failed. And then what you do is then say, "Damn! I failed again. I think I should go out and get drunk and then ponder what I should do next." And then later you go to your math book to problem solve some problems for the maths test again. That is failing slowly. You are just adding more steps or processes to learn that skill again.

To learn fast is not about doing things as quickly as possible, it is about minimizing processes to pick up a skill. And the most efficient way to pick up a skill or learn fast is to fail fast, because you will learn more from failure than if you succeeded.

Life offers many more opportunities to those who learn quickly. You will find much more success and enjoyment in life when learning new information is no longer a challenge. School, careers, hobbies, you name it and you can easily and quickly learn new facts, skills, and ideas that help you to master and succeed at them.

How many times have you thought about trying something new such as; changing careers, learning a new language, or taking on a new hobby or sport, but stopped yourself because it seemed too overwhelming and you felt it would take too long and be too hard to learn the new task.

Speed learning can change all of that. When you have the ability to learn quickly you have in turn opened a whole new world of possibilities.

Hypnosis gives you the ability to prepare your mind to learn quickly and to retain that new information. You will have the capability to ignore distractions, focus completely, and embed the new information instantly and deeply.

Opportunities are endless when you learn quickly. Success comes to those who are willing to take on new challenges and having the assurance in yourself that you can learn fast will give you the confidence to take on new and exciting opportunities. Hypnosis can give you the edge you need to learn fast.

Learning can become overwhelming and frustrating when you are inundated with distractions. Once you are able to quiet your mind you can learn much faster and learn much more. Your mind can absorb and store a much greater amount of information when you have a quiet mind. Your mind is incredibly powerful and when you are distracted by things in your environment your mind isn't being used to its full capacity.

When you gain the ability to quiet your mind and make those distractions and interruptions disappear your mind becomes a sponge and you are then able to quickly soak up new facts, skills, and ideas. Hypnosis is a simple, relaxing, and powerful tool that enables you to prepare your mind to learn fast.

Ways to Train Your Brain to Learn Faster and Remember More

You go to the gym to train your muscles. You run outside or go for hikes to train your endurance. Or, maybe you do neither of those, but still wish you exercised more.

Well, here is how to train one of the most important parts of your body: Your brain.

When you train your brain, you will:

Avoid embarrassing situations. You remember his face, but what was his name?

Be a faster learner in all sorts of different skills. No problem for you to pick up a new language or new management skill.

Avoid diseases that hit as you get older. Alzheimer's will not be affecting you.

So how to train your brain and improve your cognitive skills?

Spend Time with Your Loved Ones

If you want optimal cognitive abilities, then you've got to have meaningful relationships in your life. Talking with others and engaging with your loved ones helps you think more clearly, and it can also lift your mood.

Avoid Crossword Puzzles

Many of us, when we think of brain fitness, think of crossword puzzles. And it's true–crossword puzzles do improve our fluency, yet studies show they are not enough by themselves.

Are they fun? Yes. Do they sharpen your brain? Not really.

Of course, if you are doing this for fun, then by all means go ahead. If you are doing it for brain fitness, then you might want to choose another activity.

Work Your Memory

Twyla Tharp, a NYC-based renowned choreographer has come up with the following memory workout:

When she watches one of her performances, she tries to remember the first twelve to fourteen corrections she wants to discuss with her cast without writing them down.

If you think this is anything less than a feat, then think again. In her book The Creative Habit she says that most people cannot remember more than three.

The practice of both remembering events or things and then discussing them with others has actually been supported by brain fitness studies.

Memory activities that engage all levels of brain operation— receiving, remembering and thinking—help to improve the function of the brain.

Now, you may not have dancers to correct, but you may be required to give feedback on a presentation, or your friends may ask you what interesting things you saw at the museum. These are great opportunities to practically train your brain by flexing your memory muscles.

Learn Something New

It might sound obvious, but the more you use your brain, the better it's going to perform for you.

For example, learning a new instrument improves your skill of translating something you see (sheet music), to something you actually do (playing the instrument).

Learning a new language exposes your brain to a different way of thinking, a different way of expressing yourself.

You can even literally take it a step further, and learn how to dance. Studies indicate that learning to dance helps seniors avoid Alzheimer's. Not bad, huh?

Follow a Brain Training Program

The Internet world can help you improve your brain function while lazily sitting on your couch. A clinically proven program like BrainHQ can help you improve your memory, or think faster, by just following their brain training exercises.

Use Brain Breaks To Restore Focus.

Information overload is a real thing. In order to learn something new, our brains must send signals to our sensory receptors to save the new information, but stress and overload will prevent your brain from effectively processing and storing information.

When we are confused, anxious or feeling overwhelmed, our brains effectively shut down. You can see this happen when students listening to long, detailed lectures "zone out" and stop paying attention to what's being said.

They simply aren't able to effectively conduct that information into their memory banks, so learning shuts down. The best way to combat this is by taking a "brain break," or simply shifting your activity to focus on something new. Even a five-minute break can relieve brain fatigue and help you refocus.

Work Your Body

You knew this one was coming, didn't you? Yes indeed, exercise does not just work your body, it also improves the fitness of your brain.

Even briefly exercising for 20 minutes facilitates information processing and memory functions. But it's not just that–exercise actually helps your brain create those new neural connections faster. You will learn faster, your alertness level will increase, and you get all that by moving your body.

Now, if you are not already a regular exerciser, and already feel guilty that you are not helping your brain by exercising more, try a brain training exercise program like Exercise Bliss.

Remember, just like we discussed in #2, by training your brain to do something new repeatedly, you are actually changing yourself permanently.

Stay Hydrated.

We know we should drink water because it's good for us -- it's good for our skin and our immune system, and it keeps our body functioning optimally. But staying hydrated is also key to our cognitive abilities. Drinking water can actually make us smarter. According to one study, students who took water with them to an examination room performed better than those who didn't.

Dehydration, on the other hand, can seriously affect our mental function. When you fail to drink water, your brain has to work harder than usual.

Do Something Different Repeatedly

By actually doing something new over and over again, your brain wires new pathways that help you do this new thing better and faster.

Think back to when you were three years old. You surely were strong enough to hold a knife and a fork just fine. Yet, when you were eating all by yourself, you were creating a mess.

It was not a matter of strength, you see. It was a matter of cultivating more and better neural pathways that would help you eat by yourself just like an adult does.

And guess what? With enough repetition, you made that happen!

But how does this apply to your life right now?

Oh and by the way, I don't want you to miss this FREE guide, which can help you break free and design the life you want:

This guide will help you break your limits and overcome any challenges you have in order to live your best life.

Say you are a procrastinator. The more you don't procrastinate, the more you teach your brain not to wait for the last minute to make things happen.

Now, you might be thinking "Duh, if only not procrastinating could be that easy!"

Well, it can be. By doing something really small, that you wouldn't normally do, but is in the direction of getting that task done, you will start creating those new precious neural pathways.

So if you have been postponing organizing your desk, just take one paper and put in its right place. Or, you can go even smaller. Look at one piece of paper and decide where to put it: Trash? Right cabinet? Another room? Give it to someone?

You don't actually need to clean up that paper, you only need to decide what you need to do with it.

That's how small you can start. And yet, those neural pathways are still being built. Gradually, you will transform yourself from a procrastinator to an in-the-moment action taker.

Eat Right – and Make Sure Dark Chocolate Is Included

Foods like fish, fruits, and vegetables help your brain perform optimally. Yet, you might not know that dark chocolate gives your brain a good boost as well.

When you eat chocolate, your brain produces dopamine. And dopamine helps you learn faster and remember better. Not to mention, chocolate contains flavonols, antioxidants, which also improve your brain functions.

So next time you have something difficult to do, make sure you grab a bite or two of dark chocolate!

Learn Information In Multiple Ways.

When you use multiple ways to learn something, you'll use more regions of the brain to store information about that subject. This makes that information more interconnected and embedded in your brain. It basically creates a redundancy of knowledge within your mind, helping you truly learn the information and not just memorize it.

You can do this by using different media to stimulate different parts of the brain, such as reading notes, reading the textbook, watching a video and listening to a podcast or audio file on the topic. The more resources you use, the faster you'll learn.

Connect What You Learn With Something You Know.

The more you can relate new concepts to ideas that you already understand, the faster the you'll learn the new information. According to the book Make It Stick, many common study habits are counterproductive. They may create an illusion of mastery, but the information quickly fades from our minds.

Memory plays a central role in our ability to carry out complex cognitive tasks, such as applying knowledge to problems we haven't encountered before and drawing inferences from facts already known. By finding ways to fit new information in with preexisting knowledge, you'll find additional layers of meaning in the new material. This will help you fundamentally understand it better, and you'll be able to recall it more accurately.

Styles of Questioning That Sharpen Critical Thinking Skills

Informational gathering processes are designed to assist leaders in asking questions that facilitate the thinking skills of observation and recall. Both observation and recall thinking skills are foundational to the collection and retention of specific facts.

When questioning to promote creative and critical thinking, it is important to use employees' responses to guide subsequent questions within discussions and dialogues. Make sure to use predetermined formulated questions for dictating, channeling or directing employee responses.

Clues for posing appropriate and effective processing and probing questions are to be found in the responses given to the core questions that were asked. Because of this, leaders have to be adept listeners in order to ask appropriate processing questions that bring about quality responses.

There are seven different types of processing questions that can be used to generate higher levels of thinking. It is important to understand where and when to use each:

Verifying Questions

Verifying questions provide opportunities to cite or give evidence for ideas or specific information. Responses tend to be based on personal experiences. When verifying information, it is important to state what authorities or experts say is true, and to use a principle or generalization to support the information.

Redirecting Questions

Redirecting questions are designed to enhance personal interactions. They should be asked as often as possible within topical discussions and investigative meetings, gatherings or sessions. Redirecting questions gain a variety of responses from different employees. Two ways to redirect thinking about something is to ask: "What is another (way... thing... idea) we can bring to light to discuss about this?" And, "Will someone else offer another idea or insight on this topic?"

Refocusing Questions

Refocus questions are needed if employees are not doing enough in-depth thinking, or if are talking off the subject. To refocus employee responses, leaders may need to reacquaint them with what was said, and then restate the core question. It is important to provide specific examples when refocusing employees back onto a particular subject, idea or concept.

Clarifying Questions

Clarification is needed if responses are unclear, or if the leader feels that more appropriate language could be used to express the responder's comment, opinion or idea. Applying clarifying questions is an excellent way to build vocabulary. Appropriate clarification questions help employees define words and bring meaning to their ideas. Most miscommunication and misunderstanding is caused by not clarifying words, thoughts, concepts or ideas accurately and appropriately.

Narrowing the Focus Questions

Narrow the focus questions are used to limit the content of what is discussed or talked about. They are based on the "content characteristics" or the concepts or ideas the leader plans to address, question and discuss.

Supporting Questions

Supporting questions should be asked in order to mentally link relationships between or among evidence and statements of inference, such as cause/effect and/or prediction. Supporting questions also provide opportunities to state reasons for groupings, labels, sequences and classifications.

Recall and Verification Questions

Verification is especially critical in recalling pieces of data, information or concepts. Verification is gathered both as part of the primary material covered, as well as outside of it, in the form of past experiences, authorities, principles and generalizations.

Verifying through experiences, authorities, principles and generalizations further extends an employee's investigative skills by building additional evidence to support facts. When discussing specific facts of a particular concept or principle, the leader should ask several kinds of verifying questions so that employees become more enlightened by their understanding of the facts. For example, if an employee is asked the basic verification question, "How do you know ___?" and the employee responds, "Because I ___." it is important to follow up with another verification question that asks, "Where did you find that information?"

Informational Gathering Processes

By providing employees the opportunity to practice observing and recalling, they will better understand the thinking skills and become more aware of the types of questions they need to ask themselves when encountering situations which call for gathering and retaining information. Situations that require the observing-thinking skill must be real and representational. While situations that require the recalling-thinking skill must include questions with words that cue recollection. This at first may seem unnecessary or unimportant, however, by using cueing words, the leader assists employees in understanding how they gathered the topical content.

It also enables employees to provide sound, verifiable evidence. For example, if a leader says: "Tell me about the work task you did yesterday," employees can say how they felt about it, or talk about other tasks or assignments they liked. Further, by using the "cues" for recall, "What do you recall about your last assignment in terms of its importance?" the employee is more apt to speak directly to the details of the assignment and/or associated tasks.

Apply a Questioning Reflection Guide

There may come a time when a leader discovers that problems have surfaced when conducting a particular instructional session or meeting discussion with their employees. It may be a good policy (at least initially) to tape and transcribe at least a 5 or 10 minute interactive question and answer process. Then have another leader or peer critique the session and suggest ways to improve upon the question and answer process.

Specific things to listen for include the types of questions and sequence of questions that promote employee responses and thinking, and how to better utilize the responses. One other important thing to listen for is the pauses that occur during the "wait time" and the amount of time that passes between questions and responses.

MENTAL MODEL: THE BIOLOGICAL WORLD

Ecosystems

An ecosystem describes any group of organisms coexisting with the natural world. Most ecosystems show diverse forms of life taking on different approaches to survival, with such pressures leading to varying behavior. Social systems can be seen in the same light as the physical ecosystems and many of the same conclusions can be made.

Niches

Most organisms find a niche: a method of competing and behaving for survival. Usually, a species will select a niche for which it is best adapted. The danger arises when multiple species begin competing for the same niche, which can cause an extinction – there can be only so many species doing the same thing before limited resources give out.

Dunbar's Number

The primatologist Robin Dunbar observed through study that the number of individuals a primate can get to know and trust closely is related to the size of its neocortex. Extrapolating from his study of primates, Dunbar theorized that the Dunbar number for a human being is somewhere in the 100–250 range, which is supported by certain studies of human behavior and social networks.

Incentives

All creatures respond to incentives to keep themselves alive. This is the basic insight of biology. Constant incentives will tend to cause a biological entity to have constant behavior, to an extent. Humans are included and are particularly great examples of the incentive-driven nature of biology; however, humans are complicated in that their incentives can be hidden or intangible. The rule of life is to repeat what works and has been rewarded.

Cooperation (Including Symbiosis and Prisoner's Dilemma)

Competition tends to describe most biological systems, but cooperation at various levels is just as important a dynamic. In fact, the cooperation of a bacterium and a simple cell probably created the first complex cell and all of the life we see around us. Without cooperation, no group survives, and the cooperation of groups gives rise to even more complex versions of organization. Cooperation and competition tend to coexist at multiple levels.

The Prisoner's Dilemma is a famous application of game theory in which two prisoners are both better off cooperating with each other, but if one of them cheats, the other is better off cheating. Thus the dilemma. This model shows up in economic life, in war, and in many other areas of practical human life. Though the prisoner's dilemma theoretically leads to a poor result, in the real world, cooperation is nearly always possible and must be explored.

The Red Queen Effect (Co-evolutionary Arms Race)

The evolution-by-natural-selection model leads to something of an arms race among species competing for limited resources. When one species evolves an advantageous adaptation, a competing species must respond in kind or fail as a species. Standing pat can mean falling behind. This arms race is called the Red Queen Effect for the character in Alice in Wonderland who said, "Now, here, you see, it takes all the running you can do, to keep in the same place."

Replication

A fundamental building block of diverse biological life is high-fidelity replication. The fundamental unit of replication seems to be the DNA molecule, which provides a blueprint for the offspring to be built from physical building blocks. There are a variety of replication methods, but most can be lumped into sexual and asexual.

Hierarchical and Other Organizing Instincts

Most complex biological organisms have an innate feel for how they should organize. While not all of them end up in hierarchical structures, many do, especially in the animal kingdom. Human beings like to think they are outside of this, but they feel the hierarchical instinct as strongly as any other organism. This includes the Stanford Prison Experiment and Milgram Experiments, which demonstrated what humans learned practically many years before: the human bias towards being influenced by authority. In a dominance hierarchy such as ours, we tend to look to the leader for guidance on behavior, especially in situations of stress or uncertainty. Thus, authority figures have a responsibility to act well, whether they like it or not.

Self-Preservation Instincts

Without a strong self-preservation instinct in an organism's DNA, it would tend to disappear over time, thus eliminating that DNA. While cooperation is another important model, the self-preservation instinct is strong in all organisms and can cause violent, erratic, and/or destructive behavior for those around them.

Simple Physiological Reward-Seeking

All organisms feel pleasure and pain from simple chemical processes in their bodies which respond predictably to the outside world. Reward-seeking is an effective survival-promoting technique on average. However, those same pleasure receptors can be co-opted to cause destructive behavior, as with drug abuse.

Exaptation

Introduced by the biologist Steven Jay Gould, an exaptation refers to a trait developed for one purpose that is later used for another purpose. This is one way to explain the development of complex biological features like an eyeball; in a more primitive form, it may have been used for something else. Once it was there, and once it developed further, 3D sight became possible.

Tendency to Minimize Energy Output (Mental & Physical)

In a physical world governed by thermodynamics and competition for limited energy and resources, any biological organism that was wasteful with energy would be at a severe disadvantage for survival. Thus, we see in most instances that behavior is governed by a tendency to minimize energy usage when at all possible.

Adaptation

Species tend to adapt to their surroundings in order to survive, given the combination of their genetics and their environment – an always-unavoidable combination. However, adaptations made in an individual's lifetime are not passed down genetically, as was once thought: Populations of species adapt through the process of evolution by natural selection, as the most-fit examples of the species replicate at an above-average rate.

Evolution by Natural Selection

Evolution by natural selection was once called "the greatest idea anyone ever had." In the 19th century, Charles Darwin and Alfred Russel Wallace simultaneous realized that species evolve through random mutation and differential survival rates. If we call human intervention in animal-breeding an example of "artificial selection," we can call Mother Nature deciding the success or failure of a particular mutation "natural selection." Those best suited for survival tend to be preserved. But of course, conditions change.

Human Nature & Judgment

Language Instinct

The psychologist Steven Pinker calls our DNA-level instinct to learn grammatically constructed language the Language Instinct. The idea that grammatical language is not a simple cultural artifact was first popularized by the linguist Noam Chomsky. As we saw with the narrative instinct, we use these instincts to create shared stories, as well as to gossip, solve problems, and fight, among other things.

Grammatically ordered language theoretically carries infinite varying meaning.

First-Conclusion Bias

As Charlie Munger famously pointed out, the mind works a bit like a sperm and egg: the first idea gets in and then the mind shuts. Like many other tendencies, this is probably an energy-saving device. Our tendency to settle on first conclusions leads us to accept many erroneous results and cease asking questions; it can be countered with some simple and useful mental routines.

Trust

Fundamentally, the modern world operates on trust. Familial trust is generally a given (otherwise we'd have a hell of a time surviving), but we also choose to trust chefs, clerks, drivers, factory workers, executives, and many others. A trusting system is one that tends to work most efficiently; the rewards of trust are extremely high.

Bias from Incentives

Highly responsive to incentives, humans have perhaps the most varied and hardest to understand set of incentives in the animal kingdom. This causes us to distort our thinking when it is in our own interest to do so. A wonderful example is a salesman truly believing that his product will improve the lives of its users. It's not merely convenient that he sells the product; the fact of his selling the product causes a very real bias in his own thinking.

Pavlovian Association

Ivan Pavlov very effectively demonstrated that animals can respond not just to direct incentives but also to associated objects; remember the famous dogs salivating at the ring of a bell. Human beings are much the same and can feel positive and negative emotion towards intangible objects, with the emotion coming from past associations rather than direct effects.

Social Proof (Safety in Numbers)

Human beings are one of many social species, along with bees, ants, and chimps, among many more. We have a DNA-level instinct to seek safety in numbers and will look for social guidance of our behavior. This instinct creates a cohesive sense of cooperation and culture which would not otherwise be possible but also leads us to do foolish things if our group is doing them as well.

Narrative Instinct

Human beings have been appropriately called "the storytelling animal" because of our instinct to construct and seek meaning in narrative. It's likely that long before we developed the ability to write or to create objects, we were telling stories and thinking in stories. Nearly all social organizations, from religious institutions to corporations to nation-states, run on constructions of the narrative instinct.

Curiosity Instinct

We like to call other species curious, but we are the most curious of all, an instinct which led us out of the savanna and led us to learn a great deal about the world around us, using that information to create the world in our collective minds. The curiosity instinct leads to unique human behavior and forms of organization like the scientific enterprise. Even before there were direct incentives to innovate, humans innovated out of curiosity.

Representativeness Heuristic

The three major psychological findings that fall under Representativeness, also defined by Kahneman and his partner Tversky, are:

Failure to Account for Base Rates

An unconscious failure to look at past odds in determining current or future behavior.

Tendency to Stereotype

The tendency to broadly generalize and categorize rather than look for specific nuance. Like availability, this is generally a necessary trait for energy-saving in the brain.

Failure to See False Conjunctions

Most famously demonstrated by the Linda Test, the same two psychologists showed that students chose more vividly described individuals as more likely to fit into a predefined category than individuals with broader, more inclusive, but less vivid descriptions, even if the vivid example was a mere subset of the more inclusive set. These specific examples are seen as more representative of the category than those with the broader but vaguer descriptions, in violation of logic and probability.

Relative Satisfaction/Misery Tendencies

The envy tendency is probably the most obvious manifestation of the relative satisfaction tendency, but nearly all studies of human happiness show that it is related to the state of the person relative to either their past or their peers, not absolute. These relative tendencies cause us great misery or happiness in a very wide variety of objectively different situations and make us poor predictors of our own behavior and feelings.

Denial

Anyone who has been alive long enough realizes that, as the saying goes, "denial is not just a river in Africa." This is powerfully demonstrated in situations like war or drug abuse, where denial has powerful destructive effects but allows for behavioral inertia. Denying reality can be a coping mechanism, a survival mechanism, or a purposeful tactic.

Availability Heuristic

One of the most useful findings of modern psychology is what Daniel Kahneman calls the Availability Bias or Heuristic: We tend to most easily recall what is salient, important, frequent, and recent. The brain has its own energy-saving and inertial tendencies that we have little control over – the availability heuristic is likely one of them. Having a truly comprehensive memory would be debilitating. Some sub-

examples of the availability heuristic include the Anchoring and Sunk Cost Tendencies.

Commitment & Consistency Bias

As psychologists have frequently and famously demonstrated, humans are subject to a bias towards keeping their prior commitments and staying consistent with our prior selves when possible. This trait is necessary for social cohesion: people who often change their conclusions and habits are often distrusted. Yet our bias towards staying consistent can become, as one wag put it, a "hobgoblin of foolish minds" – when it is combined with the first-conclusion bias, we end up landing on poor answers and standing pat in the face of great evidence.

Hindsight Bias

Once we know the outcome, it's nearly impossible to turn back the clock mentally. Our narrative instinct leads us to reason that we knew it all along (whatever "it" is), when in fact we are often simply reasoning post-hoc with information not available to us before the event. The hindsight bias explains why it's wise to keep a journal of important decisions for an unaltered record and to re-examine our beliefs when we convince ourselves that we knew it all along.

Tendency to Overgeneralize from Small Samples

It's important for human beings to generalize; we need not see every instance to understand the general rule, and this works to our advantage. With generalizing, however, comes a subset of errors when we forget about the Law of Large Numbers and act as if it does not exist.

We take a small number of instances and create a general category, even if we have no statistically sound basis for the conclusion.

Tendency to Feel Envy & Jealousy

Humans have a tendency to feel envious of those receiving more than they are, and a desire "get what is theirs" in due course. The tendency towards envy is strong enough to drive otherwise irrational behavior, but is as old as humanity itself. Any system ignorant of envy effects will tend to self-immolate over time.

Influence of Stress (Including Breaking Points)

Stress causes both mental and physiological responses and tends to amplify the other biases. Almost all human mental biases become worse in the face of stress as the body goes into a fight-or-flight response, relying purely on instinct without the emergency brake of Daniel Kahneman's "System 2" type of reasoning. Stress causes hasty decisions, immediacy, and a fallback to habit, thus giving rise to the elite soldiers' motto: "In the thick of battle, you will not rise to the level of your expectations, but fall to the level of your training."

Survivorship Bias

A major problem with historiography – our interpretation of the past – is that history is famously written by the victors. We do not see what Nassim Taleb calls the "silent grave" – the lottery ticket holders who did not win. Thus, we over-attribute success to things done by the successful agent rather than to randomness or luck, and we often learn false lessons by exclusively studying victors without seeing all of the accompanying losers who acted in the same way but were not lucky enough to succeed.

Tendency to Want to Do Something (Fight/Flight,Intervention, Demonstration of Value, etc.)

We might term this Boredom Syndrome: Most humans have the tendency to need to act, even when their actions are not needed. We also tend to offer solutions even when we do not have knowledge to solve the problem.

Tendency to Distort Due to Liking/Loving or Disliking/Hating

Based on past association, stereotyping, ideology, genetic influence, or direct experience, humans have a tendency to distort their thinking in favor of people or things that they like and against people or things they dislike. This tendency leads to overrating the things we like and underrating or broadly categorizing things we dislike, often missing crucial nuances in the process.

Sensitivity to Fairness

Justice runs deep in our veins. In another illustration of our relative sense of well-being, we are careful arbiters of what is fair. Violations of fairness can be considered grounds for reciprocal action, or at least distrust. Yet fairness itself seems to be a moving target. What is seen as fair and just in one time and place may not be in another. Consider that slavery has been seen as perfectly natural and perfectly unnatural in alternating phases of human existence.

Tendency to Overestimate Consistency of Behavior (Fundamental Attribution Error)

We tend to over-ascribe the behavior of others to their innate traits rather than to situational factors, leading us to overestimate how consistent that behavior will be in the future. In such a situation, predicting behavior seems not very difficult. Of course, in practice this assumption is consistently demonstrated to be wrong, and we are consequently surprised when others do not act in accordance with the "innate" traits we've endowed them with.

Falsification / Confirmation Bias

What a man wishes, he also believes. Similarly, what we believe is what we choose to see. This is commonly referred to as the confirmation bias. It is a deeply ingrained mental habit, both energy-conserving and comfortable, to look for confirmations of long-held wisdom rather than violations. Yet the scientific process – including hypothesis generation, blind testing when needed, and objective statistical rigor – is designed to root out precisely the opposite, which is why it works so well when followed.

The modern scientific enterprise operates under the principle of falsification: A method is termed scientific if it can be stated in such a way that a certain defined result would cause it to be proved false. Pseudo-knowledge and pseudo-science operate and propagate by being unfalsifiable – as with astrology, we are unable to prove them either correct or incorrect because the conditions under which they would be shown false are never stated.

Examples of Mental Models to Practice (and Avoid)

Inversion Mental Model

The inversion perspective is one of the most powerful mental models. Rather than thinking about your desired outcome, consider the outcome you'd like to avoid.

For example, say you want to be promoted to senior marketing manager. Instead of asking yourself, "What are the top five things I could do to get promoted?" ask yourself, "What are the top 10 things that would prevent my promotion?"

Then, you'd make sure to do none of those things.

As Shane Parrish says, "Avoiding stupidity is easier than seeking brilliance." While you won't always find the answer by inverting the problem, you'll definitely improve.

Fundamental Attribution Error

We're more likely to believe someone is acting a certain way because of their character than the situation.

In other words, if your social media strategist doesn't show up to a marketing team meeting, you'll probably think, "They're flakey," not "They must have gotten stuck in traffic."

Challenge yourself to give people the benefit of the doubt. Behavior is usually situational, so your predictions of how people will act will be more accurate if you don't chalk things up to "how they are."

Hanlon's Razor

If a marketing qualified lead (MQL) goes dark at a critical point in the acquisition process, you're probably going to assume they were "kicking tires" or decided the information they had wasn't good enough to continue the conversation. Hanlon's Razor, however, asks us to "Never attribute to malice what could be explained by carelessness." In other words, it's more realistic to assume the person is busy instead.

Confirmation Bias

This is a human tendency to look for and interpret information in a way that reinforces or confirms what you already believe.

For instance, if you're confident your website's organic traffic for December will exceed its traffic from November, you might focus too much on December's promising traffic level after just the first week, and not enough on the fact that the holidays later into December often cause B2B website traffic to decrease.

To protect yourself against confirmation bias, accept the idea that your perception doesn't always (or even frequently) equal reality. Challenge yourself to find different interpretations of what's happening.

In the above example, you might think, "Is there anything to suggest our organic traffic for December will drop before the month's over? What might stand in the way of our goal?"

Being more skeptical will lead you to probe more deeply for objections -- which, in turn, will help you set more realistic expectations before it's too late.

Margin of Safety

A bridge might theoretically handle up to 15,000 pounds, but it would be wise to cap the weight limit at 14,000. It would be a major disaster if the bridge wasn't actually that strong -- and the risk isn't worth it.

The margin of safety is the idea that we should leave ourselves room for mistakes or failures. For instance, when creating your website's conversion goals, you might not count a downloaded ebook as a lead until they've responded to a follow-up email or sought more information from you, just in case they change their mind.

Think of this model as a safety net. It's better to be pleasantly surprised than proven right.

Occam's Razor

This principle states the simplest explanation is usually the correct one. If you're trying to understand what happened, develop the most basic hypothesis possible.

Opportunity Costs

Every choice comes at the cost of another. If you decide to send emails after lunch, you can't use that time to write a blog post. If you pursue one large, unpredictable lead-generation campaign, you won't have the bandwidth or the risk tolerance to pursue another at the same time.

Keep this in the back of your mind every time you're deciding what to do. What's the alternative? Are you willing to give that up?

Jealousy Tendency

There are two types of envy. The productive type is "inferiority," or the desire to raise yourself up to another person's level. Do you want to become as successful as your team's marketing director? You're motivated by this kind of envy.

The unproductive type is malicious envy, or the desire to take something valuable away from someone else -- not for your own means, but so they don't have it.

These motivators are worth remembering when, for example, you're writing website copy for your online visitors. Your visitors might be personally invested in a particular goal because they want to do as well -- or better -- than another person at their company, or beat someone else's record. Identifying your visitors' desires will help you craft landing page copy that seeks to solve their personal goals.

You should also be conscious of the jealousy tendency in your own decision-making process. While a competitive streak (inferiority envy) might benefit you in a fast-moving startup, wanting other people to fail (malicious envy) will only distract you. Overcome envy by reminding yourself of your similarities to this person, which will trigger your empathy, and avoid the temptation to sabotage them. Turn those impulses into growth opportunities: What skill or habit can you improve to get their results?

Law of Diminishing Returns

At a certain point, the incremental benefits you get from an investment get increasingly smaller. The first month you go on a diet, for example, you might lose six pounds. The second month you might lose three. The third month you might lose two.

This concept applies to marketing in several ways. First, make sure you're focusing on the most valuable activities. Let's say you've spent a week researching your buyer persona before launching a blog dedicated to them. As crucial as a detailed buyer persona is to your business, know when to call it complete. You're probably not going to double your results by spending another week sizing up your ideal buyer, and the more trivial the details get, the less those details will actually benefit your content. Instead, use that time to research a different buyer and establish multiple audience segments.

To ensure you spend your time on the things that offer the biggest returns, recognize what you need to know to be successful. Developing a brand voice and a series of calls-to-actions for your blog might be more productive than mastering the entire AP stylebook cover to cover.

There are diminishing returns to memorizing obscure details, and the sooner you notice them, the sooner you can jump on the projects that are more valuable to your business's growth.

Bayes' Theorem

This describes the probability of something happening based on potentially relevant factors. These factors include evidence from past results and current conditions that could affect a new outcome.

To give you an idea of how this theorem might look in the marketing industry, imagine you launched an email marketing campaign four months ago that had a 20% open rate. The following month, you launched a similar email marketing campaign with the goal of a 20% open rate, but instead received a 25% open rate. In the third month, your email campaign saw a 26% open rate. Then, last month, you purged your mailing list of contacts who haven't opened an email from your business in the last 60 days -- and subsequently launched another email campaign.

Given the steady increase in your open rate over the last four months, and the fact that you removed your most inactive emails from your contact list, a realistic open rate goal under Bayes' Theorem might be 30%.

Circle of Competence

We can thank Warren Buffett for this mental model. In 1996, Buffett told his shareholders, "You don't have to be an expert on every company, or even many. You only have to be able to evaluate companies within your circle of competence. The size of that circle is not very important; knowing its boundaries, however, is vital."

Concentrate on your area of expertise, and don't be afraid to say "I don't know" when you're dealing with someone else's circle of competence.

For example, a HubSpot content creator can write an article that teaches realtors how to use the inbound methodology to attract homebuyers, but she shouldn't try to write about the real estate industry itself. Realtors know far more about their customers and how the industry operates than HubSpot content creators do.

Pareto Principle

The Pareto Principle, also known as the 80/20 rule, means most results aren't distributed equally. In other words:

- 20% of the work generates 80% of the returns
- 20% of your traffic yields 80% of your leads
- 20% of features are responsible for 80% of your usage
- 20% of your time produces 80% of your results

If you can hone in on your top customers, selling activities, and so forth, you'll be dramatically more successful.

At my former company, for example, we analyzed our customers and found those who spent the most (i.e., the 20% who created 80% of our revenue) worked in HR. Once we knew that, our sales and marketing teams could target HR professionals. As a result, the company's revenue increased by 230%.

Preferential Attachment

Imagine two runners competing in a race. The first runner to pass the one-mile mark gets water and a protein bar. The slower one gets nothing.

This describes the preferential attachment, where the leader is given more resources than their competitors. Those resources give them an even greater advantage.

As a marketer, you see this effect in the lead-nurturing process. It can be tempting to spend all your time serving content to your most qualified leads. But in the process, you might be neglecting the people who are in the early stages of learning about your business, or take a bit more time to open their emails and download certain resources.

No matter how much you might "prefer" getting your furthest-along leads into the hands of a salesperson, it's important not to develop preferential attachment to these people at the expense of other website visitors.

Redundancy

Along similar lines, redundancy describes what good engineers do to put back-up systems in place to protect against failure. This drastically reduces your chances of total failure.

As a marketer, you can use this strategy to create a campaign that keeps your readers, subscribers, leads, and existing customers happy and educated while also making a bet on a brand new offering. Maybe you're promoting a huge product right now and have an ambitious lead-generation goal to hit next month. Pursue four or five smaller, low-risk content campaigns at the same time to ensure your lead-gen pipeline remains stable while also rolling out your new product.

With these mental models at your disposal, your analytical and decision making skills will exponentially improve.

The Power of Thoughts

Nothing in life is impossible, unless you think it so. Thoughts are remarkable 'packets' of energy and if you tenaciously cling to a certain thought with the dynamic willpower, there is no reason why this thought cannot manifest according to the blueprint you have created.

Earlier I briefly mentioned by explaining how a person interested in art can step up his/her abilities to excel in life. I shall now use the same example to illustrate the power of thought. An artist develops an idea of creating a painting or a drawing of a beautiful landscape.

The thought process initiates a series of ideas and the artist subsequently uses these ideas to produce the skeleton work, which allows him/her to eventually complete the final work of art according to the mental blueprint created initially. A mere thought process allows the artist to create the masterpiece!

This creation is in itself a scientific principal based on the Universal Law Of Creation. It is the source from which everything manifests. It is in us all, and it can certainly be tapped if you are just willing to give it a go. The secret is not really a secret, but it is a treasure trove within each and every one of us and we have the right to use it most efficaciously.

Is it not true that when you see someone so very happy and elated, your mind gets caught up with the cheer and you discover that there is a smile on your face?

The thoughts are so closely interweaved with the mind. If the thoughts are calm the mind is calm. In any aspect of life, be it starting a business, getting your first job or getting married, the relationship of mind and thought is foremost.

Systematically, therefore we must train and discipline the mind for right thinking and diligent activity, and thus have correct understanding of what you really want in life, and how this will add to the effectual dynamism in your quest and what you ultimately seek - your path to success and wealth will become gracious, meaningful and attainable!

People with certain qualities are almost magnetically attracted, and such qualities are called positive qualities. These qualities are present in all of us, but they are not invoked or clearly understood. We know what love, kindness, courage and joy mean, these are noble virtues, and we also recognize them as qualities we admire in others.

Despite knowing this, when we act we act compromising ideals. The reason behind this is that we are never true to our own selves - we are constantly acting and putting up a 'show' to please everyone around us, but ourselves! It is painful, demoralizing and quite agonizing not to be your true self.

Notice the changes that occur with the passage of time, and what you will truly discover is that when one can bring out into expression the fragrance of one's innate positive qualities or characteristics (of who you really are), then not only people but all the things that you have ever desired or wished for will come to you.

"As the thought, so the mind."

In order to fulfill your set goals and your dreams, it is necessary to practice what the article outlines.

The habitual inclination of our thought patterns is ultimately the deciding factor, which determines our abilities, talents and our personal characteristics. Based on this critical and vital piece of knowledge, one assumes that those lucky few have been born with the special talent you lack and fervently desire to have.

To a large extent this is true, but it has to be said that no one is born a millionaire - full stop! The valuable information lies in the art of cultivating the pattern that brings success. We are what we think we are.

It is true when Masters say that, "Your Thoughts create the environment".

- Thoughts develop personality
- Thoughts promote health
- Thoughts influence the body
- Thoughts can change and shape the future (destiny)
- Thoughts bring forth creation
- Thoughts influence the physiology and psychology of people
- Thoughts can bring success
- Thoughts can even heal the body

Watch your thoughts constantly. Your experiences and the environment have their 'seat' in thoughts.

Your suggestion, and autosuggestions via meditation and visualization techniques must be stronger than the 'thoughts, and when your actions uplift you, know that you have understood the art of controlling your thought processes.

You can accomplish anything through the power of thought. Visualization uses your imagination to allow yourself to 'picture' your success or achieving your earnest goal.

Your mental thoughts or vibrations are incredibly powerful, because the mind has a tangible connection with your thoughts and your actions. Your thoughts are subtle energies and have a strong connection to our consciousness.

Therefore, constant nourishment of positive thoughts via visualization, yoga and meditation will bring harmony, happiness, health and wealth!

Factors That Bring Inertia

First and foremost is to introspect, and this literally means that you take stock of your traits and habits.

Often, lack of self-analysis is the cause of our short fall, and it is the lack of definite, undivided effort and attention that stands in your way to progress and achievement of your desired goal.

Introspection therefore means reassessment of our mental 'block' and diagnosing deficiencies by weeding out negative tendencies in the form of habits, indecisiveness, fear, lack of confidence and so on - what we often term as failures.

It is time to reenergize so that by uprooting all these negativities from your life the true happiness with the zeal to progress becomes prominent and firmly rooted.

The greatest enemy that stops us from advancing in life other than apathy, lack of confidence and inferiority complex is FEAR. Fear will literally stop us from moving forward - in fact we will not even fulfill our very aim to succeed. The best way to combat fear is to practice deep breathing exercises, and every night mentally affirm that you are under the protection of the supreme personality of godhead, and energize your thoughts with positive feelings.

Consciously uproot the seeds of fear from within by forceful concentration upon courage, and shift your awareness to a level that allows you to fully appreciate that you are beyond any type or kind of hurting. Fear comes from the heart, so fill your heart with LOVE, and when you feel agitated relax, calm down and breathe rhythmically, relaxing with each exhalation.

Of course there is yet another problem, which I believe, is the major cause of frustration and subsequently dampening our ability to excel in life. It is, what I call 'desirous of results without the will to put in the effort'. I have personally failed because of such a negative outlook - and I am the first one to admit this openly.

Now this is where the point I made above becomes clearer. Failure, sorrow, illness and inadequacies are natural eventualities when the Law of Nature is broken.

Transgression and violation of the eternal Law of nature brings misery. As human beings we have the abilities to shape, correct and change our lives, goals and destiny.

The greatest impediment that you will ever meet in your life is your immediate environment. If anything you will have to change that - you may have noticed that I started this article sounding slightly cynical and somewhat over cautious, much less a little negative - the prime reason for this will now become apparent.

The environment that I just mentioned can be defined into two, namely the inner and the outer. It is these two fields of environment that you will have to watch out for.

All your experiences come from your mind stuff - or the inner environment (thoughts). What you perceive through all your senses from the outside will equally shape your future.

Thus the important point here is to keep watch over your thoughts. My suggestion to you is to beware of your inner environment more so than your outer environment. For example you may have stumbled upon a great home business opportunity that is potentially superb and just right for you in every aspect.

You are happy, and quite willing to give it a go...yet in retrospect something about this business 'stops' you from going ahead with it. There may be several reasons for this, but I am very curious to learn the major reason. Rest assured it cannot be the money (because it is within your budget), nor can it be a hype (because it has apparently worked for thousands with testimonials to confirm).

So what is it I wonder? Think about this point, and you will no doubt come to a favorable conclusion...and surprisingly it is, the mind stuff - the perpetrator.

To succeed in life you will have to begin by correcting your thought patterns, because it is the company of your thoughts and the affinity you have for them that will determine your fate. "Thoughts express through the physical body."

The Risk Factor

Without digressing from the subject matter, I would like to remind you what I mentioned in the early stages of the article regarding the dualistic nature of life.

Why is it that some people are so lucky and yet others fall behind in the struggle to succeed?

To answer this conclusively it is worth noting that in general majority of people have the notion that affluent people have something special which they obviously lack - This is not true as we all know, however what makes one person richer than the other is largely dependent on the choice or the decision taken, coupled with the risk(s) acknowledged through the greater understanding of the power of discrimination, and the ability to weigh and balance the scales of your intuitive faculty.

Now the risk that you take has got to be one based on the understanding that the venture you have decided to pursue has been researched thoroughly. You only embark upon taking a driving test for example once you feel that you are proficient enough to pass it and not otherwise.

Thus, the risk that you undertake in this regard has got to be what I call an informed risk. In other words, it is one where you have confidence on what you are getting yourself into, and this too is based on information source that you have searched well.

The fact that you are now reading this report is to gain the understanding on how to achieve financial success - thus this report is in a way your research tool to enable you to then implement the techniques and the tips outlined to achieve the goal. The action taken has therefore come directly from a source that can be considered authentic, valuable and genuine.

Once you feel confident to take the driving test with the guidance of the driving instructor of course, you decide to take the driving test - this is the perfect way to ensure success. I wish to redress a point made previously and it is about learning.

You must be willing to learn constantly, because to gain any skill, knowledge and power, you must be prepared to LEARN.

Commitment is the vital force which you should very much get used to from the very onset. Remember that there are certain situations that you may not have direct control to bring any foreseeable changes, which may result in much heartache.

However, this need not ever be the case because what really matters is the mechanism or the manner in which you control the situation and ultimately how well you react to it.

The trouble with us is that we tend to live in the past and in the future at the same time. When our mental faculty becomes over burdened we become discouraged.

The load is too heavy for the mind, so we must restrict the load. When we have too much to do at one time, we should at once stop our activities. The clock ticks on at a regular pace, it cannot tick twenty four hours away in 60 seconds, nor can you do in one hour what you can do most effectively in twenty four hours. Live for the now, and the 'future' will take care of itself.

Do not be greedy and above all do not burn yourself out by 'wanting' to become a millionaire!

The tables have turned around, more and more people are resorting to a simple back to basics lifestyle - without so many luxuries and fewer worries.

The dualistic concept of nature is prevalent everywhere - you cannot prosper if you write out cheques without having credible funds or credit (deposit) in your bank account, sooner or later you will run out of money.

Without peace of mind, the likely hood of running out of 'steam', happiness, calmness and strength you will become 'bankrupt' mentally, emotionally, spiritually and physically drained. What a pity it will have all been to come to a point of utter desolation!

This is when you must dwell on the power within, and mentally affirm your purpose in life; you may want to go through some pleasant experience so that you forget your worries completely. The point is do not take anything too seriously, enjoy what you have and be happy with what is your due.

What You Must Avoid

It is natural that when the unforeseen happens we are far more likely to react in a negative way. However this need not be so, the article reveals ways to achieve your goal harmoniously and diligently.

The following are some pointers that will be most helpful:

- When things go wrong do not overreact. Think positively and calmly.
- Do not be over judgmental, and over critical.
- Try not to ignore a bad situation, beware of the comfort zone.
- Wisdom and strength alone can help you overcome much of life's imminent problems.
- Tackle problems head on.
- Avoid greed and conceit of any kind.

There is a business ethics and a businessman should practice this ethics. Those who are strictly honest and truthful will flourish in business. Let us once again consider art as an example to highlight what has been discussed thus far. As we all know we have innate powers -

within each and everyone of us lies the storehouse of latent energy bursting to be 'awakened'.

Let us assume that you have the creative power, and that being an artist for example you can virtually paint and draw any subject or theme.

Fair enough, it is obvious that you have considerable talent as not all artists have this ability. Since you are aware of this, you may assume that because your artwork is good it has good potential to be sold. True, but let us consider all factors that need to be taken into account a step at a time.

- You may be a very good artist, but if your work does not get noticed and appreciated, it is of no real benefit. It is important therefore that your work gets noticed (through maximum exposure) and the way to do this is get your name established.

  This requires that you contact the right sources and approach artists who have been through the 'same' learning curve as it were to reach the path of prosperity. You must take into consideration competition that may exist in your chosen field. You must prepare a good foundation - this can be done using the information within this article.

- Your artwork may be exceptionally beautiful, but without understanding the dynamics of the market place your work may not blossom.

- From your personal perspective your work may seem to have great potential. However, it is relevant to appreciate the views of the general public - in other words your potential buyers.

Do not get into the rut that most do, "hearing what we want to hear" this is a type of preconditioning that can bring untold misery.

- You must look into other areas to develop your potential. Expand on subject category/theme, use of various different types of media (e.g. acrylics, oils. Mixed media etc.), deciding on how to promote your work, you may even want to sell originals or reproduce prints perhaps... The possibilities are endless, the question is how determined you are in your quest to succeed.

The psychology of success depends on number of factors, but the one I believe that is most vital is self-belief. Most people never get the first stage of success because they lack this characteristic, which is essential.

Such conditioning often stems from your personal experiences, but the causative factor is environment, which has already been discussed. Though it is good to be cautious about anything that you do in life, it is equally essential that you do not get tangled into the technicalities of the 'process', but rather focus on the benefits and the ultimate reward that it yields.

Dedicate your goal to achieving success by implementing the five cardinal words beginning with the letter D to your success, namely Devotion, Discrimination, Discipline, Determination and Duty.

There is no harm in raising questions regarding proposals that come your way or even business opportunities you intend pursuing. So long as these questions afford all the answers and that you decide to follow through considering all the factors, then it is all well and good.

However, when your questions defeat the very purpose of your inquiry then it becomes a 'vicious cycle'.

Why, what, where, when, who are words that we often use to ascertain information about everything in life including business ventures - thus giving rise to questions.

The question with the word why is a necessity for it will help us draw a perfect conclusion and help us overcome doubts. The problem with this is that if you are not clear about your goal(s), then the very question why you wish to even pursue the venture becomes meaningless.

What you must consider are probable long-term goals, benefits and how your first step to wealth and success will enable you to enjoy greater heights.

The Inevitable Mistakes

As human beings we are very restless - we often become overwhelmed with joy, success or gratification. It is so very important to maintain your calm during such events, because excitement can lead to problems, of which one is over spending.

That said, it is also quite important to realize that success may just 'knock' you back, in that you may become complacent and 'decide' not to do much, because you 'have it all'.

This is a terrible phase that you could ever possibly get into, and one you must consciously be aware of at all times. However, the one thing that you must beware of is the ego complex - do not let your ego become an impediment in your endeavor to attain wealth.

The best medicine to avoid ego is to conserve energy. The energy that has been generated and conserved, unless it is directed into the right channels, it will be catastrophic.

We must control our urges, and this is where the art of practicing balance in life becomes an essential tool to your success. Idle talk is one single factor that can destroy your desire to succeed.

Remember, that people around you and the company you have will determine your future success

- you may waste precious time, but those around you will make it even worse, they will contribute to overall wastage of your own time.

Thus as the saying goes, 'like attracts like' should be the maxim, and above all use your common sense all the time, and only do that which produces positive results.

Being systematic too will help avoid confusion and annoyances, which can both, have an adverse effect in your business venture and goals. Do not take on board work that may set you back.

Try to evaluate the situation, paying much importance on priorities - do not procrastinate, do not waste time and most of all do not waste your precious energy. If you act thoughtfully then time will be managed most efficiently.

The Power of Positive Thinking

People who are blessed with the quality to energize their thought process with mammoth degree of positivity are sure enough to achieve the success in all fronts in professional and social life. They are classified as people with a positive frame of mind and do not get provoked and indulge in any sort of mental block. They are also like many others; but only difference is that they do not delve much on their weaknesses and do not blame their luck for any failures. They consider the failures as a stepping stone which shows them the path of success. This is one side of the coin. The opposite side is also prevalent. That means there are people who always focus attention to their past mistakes, murmur, curse the environment and situations for failures. These thoughts make their minds distract from positivity and abundance of failures will always rattle their inner self.

You have to remember that you are always better than what you are. You have to have full trust on your ability and intelligence. Your body is like one of the highly acclaimed machines and your brain deserves to be a critical asset. You can definitely accept the challenges of the surroundings with all these combinations. To make these all happen, a personality trait which is a very important factor for anybody, to amplify - is known as attitude. This attitude helps you to induce the power of thinking in a very positive way and this eight letters word can create a magic wind for you. As per Winston Churchill, "An attitude is a small ingredient, but makes a lot of difference in your life."

Power of thoughts:

Any action is a reflection of thought process which is guided by a positive or a negative thought. You will become a successful person, when you are influenced by lifting up your thoughts. The research data shows that the working pattern of your body and your thoughts have interconnection. If you are endowed with a positive frame of mind and thoughts, you will be able to lift your spirit. Contrarily, if your mind is always hovered with the thoughts of failures, surely you would encounter the same only. In my professional life, I come across different types of personalities and I have the privilege to segregate the intellectual lot with haughty nature, and ample money power versus the lot with less materialistic power, but with intensive positive attitudinal perch of mind. And, to the best of the best of my knowledge, I opine that the second lot makes history and always smile in their lives beatifically.

You take the instance of the environment either of office or work, all your acts will be governed by thoughts. Depending on the gravity of your acts for any assignment, you will be able to judge your performance. The level of performance will enhance when the acts will be influenced by a positive attitude. You will be able to raise the output beyond the expected level because of the constructive behaviour and so consequence of the results therefore, will be always positive.

The success is not a derivative of any lose efforts. It is a structural and a continuous process of development of various skills and knowledge and when bestowed with positive thoughts, right actions are guaranteed to happen. So, for advancement in life, fill up your mind with positive, productive and enriching thoughts. This will ensure you for a noticeable difference in your attitude towards the life.

Sole searching:

Many a time, in your life, you feel yourself less enthusiastic and ponder on anxieties caused due to various perceptions which may or may not have any relationship with your career, social life or materialistic despondency. But, such behaviour is quite radical. Because, even otherwise your brilliancy is undoubtedly beyond questionable, the negative thoughts may crop up in your mind just because of above situations. Whatever the positive frame of mind you possess, negative thoughts as stated above, will destroy the energy of your inner self and you will be under shackles of despair. Please remember that nothing is achievable easily and so you have to toil excessively and endlessly to earn other peoples support services, their co-operation and good wishes

This is just a guide line, but to energize your inner self with the power of positive thought, you have to continuously introspect till the time; you recognize the truth of its importance.

Build up yourself:

A normal person of average caliber, even otherwise possesses several abilities which are up to the mark with respect to any prevailing standard may require to invest for his overall growth. You have to continuously upgrade your skills, knowledge, and keenness to float in the corporate jungle. Always concentrate on the job which you like and know more about the same. This keenness will only bring more colour to your life and your career graph will zoom.

Plan, follow and improve:

If your planning is perfect and accurate, the accomplishment of a job will be far above than the expected result. To do this, you have to be extremely effective to master the techniques of the job. You have to have enough skills to undertake the job. The role of planning, in this case, is a very important thing. If the planning is foolproof, the results cannot be haywire. A person, who does not recognize the importance of the planning, will be clueless and cannot reach to a desired destination. Here comes the perspective of the attitude. Without this personality trait, it is extremely difficult to achieve any success in the life. The success is like a war which is full of mirth and despondency. If your planning is strong enough and devised with scientific approaches, then the success cannot delude you.

It is very essential to dwell on the strengths in stead of the weaknesses. No one should sulk on what they do not have, rather a concentration of the entire focus is to be put forward what we have. The celebrities from all round the corner never brood in their limitations as their attitudinal behaviour will always guide them to the path of positive thinking. And this character alone will be benevolent for their success in their lives. Always keep an attitude to constantly upgrade yourself because there is no substitute for the same. By indulging for self development, you will be in a position to improve upon your performance in any field. No sooner, you will show complacent, downfall will start and you will not be in a position to filter further.

Attitude:

This can be spelt as follows:

A = Attribute - to be positive.

T = Try - to change if the attitude is negative

T = Total control - to negate your negative thoughts.

I = Instinct - to use to visualize the positive, even in adversity.

T = Think - to start every thing with positive and constructive approach.

U = Understand - all your inherent strengths.

D = Develop - your conscious to achieve the best.

E = Energize - your inner self to influence outer self to be always positive.

You have to remember that in a professional as well as social environment, your attitude will affect other people and what they think of you. In today's' competitive working environment, when you have to work in a team, your attitude is one of the main criteria for your success. Without a balanced attitude, it will be tricky for you to overcome the obstacles which are developed off and on. So, thoughts are to be sensitized and to be added with fantasies to eradicate the negative emotions. By practicing this hypothesis, gradually, mind will be energized to pursue the positive aspect of the thoughts. This will, in turn, become a habit and transform to the attitude.

Attitudinal behaviour and its impact on career:

This personality trait is very important determinant, at the start of your professional career, because when you appear for interview, the interviewers gauze subtly your this quality. Because, they know that they can train you to their job requirement, but it is extremely difficult for them to change your attitude.

You will be able to conquer any obstacles, if you have a positive attitude. This positive attitude will be able to blossom your inherent quality to focus your attention to the brighter side of any things.

In my professional career of marketing, as a departmental head since long, I always encourage on coaching of my people to take out the best possible output from them. I have noticed that if a person has a positive attitude and the ability of "can do confidence," he will, by and large, achieve the success even he is weak in some sphere of the knowledge. On the contrary, may be, some people are very brilliant but totally engrossed with a negative attitude, they are the maximum sufferers. In today's' global competitive arena, the companies are always in search of the people, who show the immense power of positive attitude in all spheres.

Mostly, all the companies are now conducting psychometric analytical tests to measure the candidates attitude and then conclude about the potentiality of the success of a candidate. Individually, they are capable to exhibit tremendous performance when they are blessed with the positive frame of mind. You have to become a master of the mind but not its slave. By doing this, you will be able to control your mind and will be in a position to always concentrate on positive things of the surroundings.

Keep away from negative:

The life is completely full of mysteries of successes and failures. Everyone has to face this naked truth. Failures doom the strengths of a person and develop negative consequences. Whatever they see, it will be full of darkness. The famous couplet of "Genesis" of the Bible says that during the creation of the universe, the first thing, God said "Let there be a light" because the total universe was under the clutch of the darkness. God never said, "Let there be darkness." In the similar way, in our day to day life, we have to always encounter the darkness with a light. If you are calm and quiet, and maintain a positive frame of mind even in your disastrous state of your life, a habit of positiveness will grow which will enable you to think always to see the brighter side of the life only. I would like to put forward a classic example of positive attitude which many of us know very well. Mr. Iswarchandra Vidyasagar, the eminent scholar, was summoned one day by her mother to meet. When he reached to the river Damodar during late evening, he could not find any boat because of heavy tidal conditions. But he had made up his mind to meet her mother by hook or by crook and so, he ignored the fanatic condition of the river. He swam and reached to his house late night to touch the feet of her mother. What a positive attitude he showed! This example glorifies, how to steer away the darkness and the negativity of the life.

Attitude V/s Success:

An attitude and a success, both are hand in gloves. The success is directly proportional to the positive attitude. You can never dream a success without a positive attitude. "I can do" attitude only can plan your actions into reality and results. Please keep in mind that any success is not easily achievable. Mind boggling efforts, pain-staking work, eradication of negative thoughts, and tremendous perseverance are required to feel the stepping stone of success. In your this endeavour, you will come across resources crunch, negative criticism from peers and friends, hurdles of circumstances but keep your all positive thoughts intact for your motivation to perform the best and success will be guaranteed.

There is no magic wind for the success. It comes to you automatically, if you exert your best efforts with brimming confidence of mind. When you engage yourself in any purposeful action, maximize your potentialities, concentrate and focus all your attentions to the actions with constructive and positive thoughts, you will always find your missions completed.

As a marketing coach in my present employment, I impart training to the young engineers for their career upbringing. To make them aware of the fundamental principles of the products development versus marketing operations, I profusely teach them the importance of the attitude. During the initial six months of probation training, I ensure them to concentrate on positive thoughts, or else I make them understand that they will face enormous problems in achieving their career goals.

Further, many people think that positive thoughts are the domain of some particular persons. But, it is not correct. Even, if you are average qualified, have mediocre brain, and aged, you can always learn and practice the power of positive thoughts. To maintain the thought process in a positive direction, you need not be over qualified or have super brain power. It is only a matter of habit that how you shut the door of your mind and prevent the entry of any negative thoughts. This is the main and important quality which is required to sharpen the skill to think always positive. It is true that negative thoughts cannot be erased, but if you put layers after layers of positive thoughts into your mind, then the same becomes a habit. Once you are habituated to discharge your duties with positive thoughts, the influence of all stored negative thoughts become insignificant.

Change With Your Brain In Mind

What you pay attention to create experiences. Your experiences generate beliefs. Your beliefs drive your actions. Your actions produce results.

When you want to make a change in your life, you are in effect making a decision to begin paying attention to something different, something new, something that may be uncomfortable. Attending to something new generates new experiences, which can eventually drive different results.

Making a positive change in your life is first about focusing your attention on new experiences.

As humans beings our five senses bring us a continuous stream of information. We are constantly in some combination of hearing, seeing, tasting, touching, and smelling our environment.

However, because of the way the brain works, most of what our senses take in never makes it to conscious awareness.

Important fundamentals about your brain that influences your behavior and how your brain responds to change:

First, your brain is the largest consumer of energy in your body. When you are really focused on something, your brain is consuming a tremendous amount of energy.

Second, because humans evolved in a world where energy was scarce and you didn't always know where your next meal was coming from, conserving energy evolved as a fundamental survival principle.

Third, as the largest consumer of energy, your brain evolved to conserve energy wherever possible. One of the ways the brain conserves energy is discarding if you will, inputs from your senses that your brain has previously identified as non-threatening or routine.

Fourth, ignoring or paying little attention to previously identified sounds, sights, etc., allows your brain to be ready to pay attention to things that are new and potentially food, or something that sees you as food. Remember fifty thousand years ago, you didn't necessarily know where your next meal was coming from, but equally important you didn't necessarily know when you would encounter something that wanted to make you their next meal.

So in order to be able to quickly recognize a threat in your environment and to conserve energy, your brain wants to be in stable, well-known places. For example, your brain wants the sounds it hears to be routine, repetitive sounds it hears everyday so it can be ready to attend to unusual noises like a lion's roar or someone approaching. As an interesting aside, our brains are wired so that loud noises go directly to the part of the brain that controls the fight or flight response, which is why we jump at loud noises, even sometimes when we know they are coming.

Because focused attention increases the already large amount of energy your brain consumes, your brain is also hard wired to quickly incorporate the new and the novel into the common and routine. Continuing our examples of sound, have you ever noticed how people who have lived next to a railroad or subway for a long time seem to barely notice the train roaring by? How they get up to steady a plate about to vibrate off the table all the while continuing their conversation without pause or even looking at the passing train; just automatically raising their voices so they can be heard, while you are totally focused on how loud the train is.

One of the ways our brains help us to reduce how much we have to pay attention to things is through habits. Once you have a routine down in the morning, you don't really think about it. You are probably thinking about something else while you go through the motions of what you do every morning.

This can be true of even complex tasks. Think about how much attention and focus it required when you were learning how to drive a car and how soon the act of driving no longer dominated your attention. You have probably heard someone say, or maybe you have said, "I don't mind the long drive into work. It gives me time to think about what I have to get done that day."

Or think about those first few days at a new job or a new school when everything was new and unusual and how much conscious thought and effort it took while you made your way through a new environment. Then contrast that with what it is like today now that the environment is no longer new and getting to work or school is routine. Then think about how annoyed you get when something takes you out of your routine.

Becoming accustomed to our environment happens naturally. You don't really decide, it just happens.

Your brain wants to free up your conscious mind from routine events, avoiding the energy drain they would cause, so that you are ready to attend to the unusual, the important, the life threatening, or life sustaining.

The important point here is that your brain has evolved over time to classify much of what you experience every day into non-important routine events that don't require a lot attention, so that you are free to attend to new or important experiences.

However, just because the brain wants to make sure you can attend to new events doesn't mean it likes the new or the novel. In fact, it is just the opposite, which we will explore next.

When you want to make a change in your life, you are in effect making a decision to begin paying attention to something different, something new, something that may be uncomfortable.

There are three important points here.

- One, your brain doesn't want new, it wants the familiar, the low energy experiences that it knows and feels safe about.
- Two, your brain is going to compare new experiences with what it knows and look to avoid repeating the experience, especially if your conscious mind thinks of the new experience as negative.
- Third, in spite of point number 2, if the experience is repeated enough, it begins to incorporate that experience, even negative ones, into the familiar so that it doesn't burn up so much energy.

When you want to make a change in your life, recognize that your brain is wired to not like change. The status quo is safe. Change is risky. Change takes energy. Your brain wants to conserve energy. The brain wants certainty. Change is uncertain.

Like an over protective relative or friend who gets anxious when you want to do something new, our brains will experience discomfort with new.

So knowing that, are there ways you can help your brain and yourself get beyond the threatening, energy intensive new to a place where change becomes the safe low energy familiar?

Here ways you can align your thoughts and actions with how your brain works.

Social Connections - Connecting with people builds connections in your brain

Some have written that time spent connecting with others is more important than even maintaining a good diet.

As humans, we are first and foremost social beings. The brain rewards us when we make quality social connections. When we connect with others in a mutual exchange of sharing emotions, goals, and ideas the brain releases oxytocin, a chemical that gives us a great sense of pleasure.

Find others who share your interest in the change you want to make. Seek out those, who like you, have set out to change their life, to learn a new skill, to start a new business, or to start a new chapter in their lives. Sharing your experiences and listening to others share their experiences helps your brain moderate its perception of the change as a threat.

These rewards further strengthen the connections you are building in your brain and provide a positive motivation to continue. Learners are most motivated when they possess the belief that they can succeed at learning.

Downtime - Give yourself a break

Finally, one activity we all need is sufficient time to refresh our brains. Make sure to spend some time being non-goal focused. Like your muscles after exercise, our neural circuits benefit from a period of recovery.

Quiet time is also an important factor for solving complex problems. When we are constantly attending to the electronic imperatives of computers and mobile devices, our conscious brain can be too busy to notice the solutions our quieter, subconscious is sending up to us. Too much constant on the go and you miss the "Aha!" moments that pop into your thoughts when you aren't really thinking about anything in particular.

Expectation - Set your expectations to what you want to experience in the world and you will notice more of it.

Have you ever noticed how after you decide to buy a new electronic device or maybe a new car, you suddenly begin to see them everywhere?

They didn't magically appear. They were always there, however you tend not to notice things unrelated to your interests.

What changed is related to how making a decision to do something acts on your perceptual processes. It actually affects how neurons fire in response to what we see. The object of your decision now has your interest and the perceptual part of your brain starts to respond when it recognizes something related to your new interest.

Instead of the "nothing to see here, let's move on" type of response that may not even make it your conscious awareness, your brain responds with a "hey there has been some interest here, better send it up to have it checked out".

Things we may see or hear about real estate investing may barely register in our conscious awareness until we decide we are interested in real estate investing.

In addition to paying more attention to real estate investing, your brain will automatically begin to compare and contrast this new interest with previous experiences looking for something familiar.

Your brain uses previous experience to set expectations for what your perceptual circuits should be looking for to send up to our conscious awareness. Expectations alter how you experience events. Your inner expectations influence what information you take notice of in the world.

When the expectation is negative, your brain primes itself to sense evidence of negative outcomes. Once primed your brain will focus on every hint of the negative, real or imagined, and ignore or minimize the positive.

You can prepare the perceptual part of your brain by where you direct your attention.

Set your expectations to what you want to experience in the world and you will notice more of it. Repetition and Goals can help you get your expectations focused in the right direction.

Goals - Make the complex a lot of simple

To help make things more automatic, complex learning tasks are better when they are divided into smaller, more manageable portions.

A change that is divided into a sequence of smaller, simpler tasks is less likely to cause stress from uncertainty, fear, or ambiguity and thus increase your chances for success.

Our brains are wired to immediately detect changes or possible errors in the environment and to send strong signals to alert us to anything unusual, or unknown. This error alert mechanism in the brain is closely connected to the brain's fear circuitry. Error detection causes us to act more emotionally and more impulsively.

Our thinking can be easily overwhelmed and flooded with error signals when we are faced with situations of uncertainty, rejection, unfairness, or ambiguity.

To use learning to drive as an example, most of us started slowly someplace where there is little traffic. Our brain was busily making new connections between the parts of the brain that handle vision, motor controls, and making decisions. The increasing level of comfort you felt as you learned to drive was a result of the increasingly stronger connections developing within your brain.

Imagine how your brain would respond if for your first driving lesson, your driving instructor drove you to the on ramp of a busy fast-moving 8 lane freeway and told you to take the drivers seat, get on the freeway, and immediately get into the fast lane.

Yet, sometimes in our zeal for self-improvement and personal development, we in effect try to jump right into the fast lane.

Set smaller goals that are specific and well defined so you know what action to take. You will also have more success with goals that are time-defined instead of vague references to the future: two months as opposed to sometime next year. They should be measureable so you can track your progress and challenging enough to provide a level of engagement but not so challenging as to produce stress and invoke error signals.

Breaking down large tasks into smaller portions also helps you to leverage Expectation and Repetition. By taking incremental steps, you can leverage the brains desire to automate tasks. As you build your expertise, your brain is developing the connections that allow the brain to perform functions related to your new skills in a less stressful, lower energy, more automated fashion.

The brain also uses past experiences to set expectations for future events. The brains experience of success through gradual steps helps set the expectation for more success which primes your perceptual system to look for confirmations of future success, not confirmations of past failure.

Setting the right goals can help you create and sustain the belief that you can succeed, but you also need time to focus.

Focus - Make the most of the limited time you have

Your conscious awareness and the brain circuits that support it are easily distracted by the endless incoming sensory inputs your brain is processing. It requires immense energy to maintain your focus on just one thing.

A distraction is a signal that something in your environment has changed and that you have to pay attention to it. The key phrase here is "have to". Attending to change signals in the environment is automatic. Your brain is hard wired to alert you to anything that might be a threat.

Focus is much easier in environments where you can tune out distractions. For some this will be a quiet place, but for others silence is in itself a distraction and they focus best in an open, public place like a coffee shop.

When you focus on a single task, you are making deeper connections within your brain. Focus helps move what you are learning into long-term memory so it can be more easily retrieved when needed.

Research has shown that your peak period for focused work is only one to two hours per day. If those hours are in an environment where you are constantly being distracted, you are wasting valuable time. Our peak time of day also tends to be either early in the morning or late at night. Find the best time for you.

Repetition - The more you do something, the less energy your brain needs to do it

Making a change, from something simple like shopping in a new grocery store to learning a musical instrument, is a process of making new connections in your brain.

As you learn new tasks or skills, different patterns of neurons in various parts of the brain begin to make a connection. The more times a task is repeated the stronger those connections become. The stronger they become, the more automatic the task becomes, reducing the energy required of our conscious awareness (think learning to drive a car).

Remember your brain wants to automate as much of what it does as possible so it can be free to pay attention to changes in your environment that may represent a threat.

Simple tasks can become automatic in as little as three repetitions, however complex tasks may take many hours. Highly complex tasks, like developing an expertise in some endeavor, are an ongoing process that requires several thousands of hours of practice and reflection.

The kind of change you are contemplating or trying to make is likely of the more complex variety and you can easily become overwhelmed by it. That is where the right goals can help.

Visualization - Seeing is connecting

The brain circuitry used to physically do something is the same pathways used when we imagine it. The brain does not distinguish between real and imagined events.

Rehearsing mentally can prepare mental circuits in ways similar to actually doing something. Visualization can also help to resolve fears when you "see" yourself making the change or doing the tasks you want to accomplish. Visualization also leverages the power of repetition to build and strengthen neural connections.

There are three important aspects of visualization.

- First, it has to be correct. Visualizing something incorrectly only services to strengthen incorrect behavior.
- Second, the more vivid and detailed you can make the visualization the more connections it creates in the brain.

- Third, visualization is most effective in short durations spaced over time. It is better to spend 3 minutes a day for 5 days rather than visualizing something for 20 minutes in one day.

Words of Affirmation & Power of Affirmation

Words of affirmation are so prevalent, important, and powerful but yet subtle, so subtle that we don't even notice it being the underlining governor in our minds and in our life's experiences. Words of affirmation have conditioned us in ways that most people have not even considered in their adult years.

For instance, we have been conditioned from school, through things like mathematics, to create problems for ourselves over and over again. Through all of the different equations we had to find to solve all of the many problem-solving questions that math teachers gave their students, and still are giving them today... we have been conditioned to create problems for ourselves. This can be turned into good if it forces us to find solutions to where our attention and focus are more steered toward solutions but unfortunately with the mental overwhelming of mind activity, and lack of concentration, we focus more on the problems and create more problems for ourselves.

But on a subconscious level we have seen the words "Problem Solving" so much in our youth that we have hardwired our brains to search out and notice problems just to solve them for the chemical rush of being right, which can put us in a state to refining our skills in that area. But most schools, at the same time of flooding students with problems to solve, have numerous intellectual commitments, assignments, test, exams, essay papers and many other things that keep the mind at a constant turbulent multi tasking state.

This unfortunately makes it harder for kids to realize and expand their talents and concentration skills and interest because they are mentally tired from all of the requirements of problem solving. Whenever things seem to be going right, the minds is conditioned to seek out a problem that is hidden and the world respond and bring us situations to deal with that we interpret as problems to solve.

Not a lot of attention was put into concentration, contemplation, mental rehearsal and imagination. More of the attention was on problem solving and measuring apartness and separation and calculating reactions and implementing solutions. This can be effective if used rightly but we fail to ascend from the problematic limited way of thinking to the expressions of creativity, abundance and infinite possibilities ways of thinking.

This same mentality has creeped into the minds of most adults and the word job is the new school for problem solving mechanisms using some form of "work". We have forgotten unconditional love and hardwired our families to be computers to survive in this tough financial problem solving society.

The love has been striped out of families for survival because on an unconscious level we have prepared and organized our brains to seek out problems to solve without us even knowing it which cripples the idea of enhancing and refining our skill to strategies and master challenges in a subconscious and automatic implicit way for a desired outcome using concentration and pure powerful thinking.

We seem to have been stuck in a problem-seeking mode and when we get overwhelmed we go on vacation with the family to catch up on expressing love and life. Our spirit guide knows that it needs love to continue life's full expression rather our minds allow it or not. This is what creates the imbalance in our wholeness because our intent in mind is different than our intent in heart.

We have been programmed to survive and as parents we sometimes see our kids as motivation to survive which works for a while but you naturally need to Love, Love and Love first. Seek the way of the creator first and your needs will be meet. But we have been delivered from youth, certain problematic words of affirmation in our DNA unconsciously, that has implicitly become our automatic behaviors and ways of thinking.

Love and life has become secondary to surviving. What a tiresome way of living life. Oh lets survive by getting a job, paying bills and keeping a roof over our heads, food on the table and clothes on our backs and then when we have time we will pay attention to one another.

The people who master these problem-solving techniques become our leaders in government, education, media and mainstream. They set the tone and reinforce a system that creates a world of chaos and limitations because all the problems are based on limitation, apartness, labels and division and we have identified our selves and who we think we are with our ability to solve problems.

This is why the entrepreneur world is so big because there are so many problems and an entrepreneur is no more than some one who solves problems and address needs for people for a profit. Helping the needy has become life's purpose because the parasite exists in the minds of the poverties but Christ consciousness is the keys to full fill this gap. There are many needs in this world because the adversary, through mind, has kept the knowledge away from us of how to create abundance instead of limitations.

From the jump early school systems painted the picture of education that they wanted us to see so that we will live a life of trading time in for ends meet. They know time is limited, which is a problem for us, if that is what you have to rely on to survive. They have mentally equipped us to be in a rat race of specific problems that we had no part in creating. We are at the bottom of the employee food chain acting out as parts of the equation that the successful problem solver has put in place and created a business out of.

This may seem all to coincidental or distant for a lot of people but I assure you if you look deeper you will see that the underlining words of affirmation that has been hardwired in our intellect corresponds equally to what we believe and what we manifest in our present reality.

The very few wealthy people in the world have surpassed this limited way of thinking and they see that there are no limitation problems in the now. They see what most people label as problems as challenges that they have learned to graciously overcome. They have implanted into their memory program a new set of words of affirmation. Affirmations are so effective in our lives rather we are affirming abundance or limitation. Whatever you organize your brain to tell you is what it will produce.

Most people do not realize that words of affirmation works on an unconscious level in a very big way. Our unconscious thoughts produce measurable changes in our physiology but most people are not aware of the unconscious thinking in their heads. If you are worrying about some future moment in the back of your head and you can't consciously remember exactly what it is your worrying about at that moment, you are affirming some form of words that have been planted in your subconscious.

We have been conditioned by time to treat the present moment as a problem or an obstacle that needs to be over come. Some how we have gotten stuck in the "oh no its another problem" mode. The idea of no problems but only challenges and solutions starts to make your brain works differently but that different feeling is the unknown. The familiar is so seductive because we can relate to what a problem feels like.

Peace Affirmations

We have not hardwired our brain to experience a reflection of paradise with ultimate peace and only love because of the parasite in our mind that keeps the past alive. Every time we think there is no problems, the body and mind conditioned past finds a problem. Christ tried to present us another way of living when he implied to his followers that they should live like nature. He said look at the lilies and the birds. See how they grow with no stress or toil. You can live like that too.

The only way we can live like that is through the thoughts we choose to focus on in this moment. In order to live like the lily your thoughts has to be natural and clear like the growth of the lily. We must allow life to be freely with an attitude of peace and wholeness no matter what the present circumstance. This action creates a reaction of peace in the future.

The karma for a natural flower is natural beauty because it's action and reaction is natural with no distress and rooted in love. It takes in just enough solar energy and water and the roots grow and create beauty on the outside through the creators love. The only thing that gets in the way of us living our lives so peacefully like the Lilly and the bird is fear in the human mind. We have lost control of it do to the conditioning of problem solving words of affirmation.

We have to gain control of our subconscious memory system and alter our attention to abundant words of affirmation. We have been condition by school for most of our early years so more than likely you have to unlearn some things you've been taught. Whatever words of affirmation you have plant in your mental garden, will be the same words that grows in your physical world as manifestation of things and reality and now is the time to pluck up roots and plant new seeds.

Then the new seeds of abundance have to become deeply rooted and implicit so that it can be automatic. Peace and love becomes second nature and all other needs are added as a result of producing compassion now.

Words of Affirmations effect life in many different areas

- Affirmations for healing
- Affirmations for abundance
- Affirmations for wealth
- Self Confidence Affirmations
- Positive Thinking Affirmations
- Affirmations of Happiness
- Affirmations for Money
- Affirmations for Relationships
- Audio Affirmation

Pluck up the negative words of affirmations that creeped in unconsciously through

- Affirmations of Problems
- Affirmations of Limitation
- Affirmations of Disease
- Affirmations of Anger
- Affirmations of Fighting
- Affirmations of Surviving
- Affirmations of Fear
- Affirmations of Victim

These words of affirmations come in through many ways- from what we read, what we see on televisions and the news, what we learned in school, what we experience at work, what we hear on radio, what we perceive from others, what we see in hospitals, what we experience through drama and chaotic episodes, what we hear in church and what we learn from surviving life situations.

Our conscious mind is like a compass and it guides our subconscious by the words of affirmations we hold in our mind and make more real than anything else. Words are thoughts externalized and as a man think in his heart, so is he. This explains why we become what we have affirmed implicitly. Our spirit guide has to plant new affirmations but first it must make unconscious negative affirmations conscious so that we can recognize it and be in a position to choose a different way of affirming our experiences continuously.

We are constantly affirming reality through the words of affirmations we have stored in our storehouse of affirmations. If we have affirmed going to school, getting good grades and graduating and going to college then working for 8 hours a day, 40 hours a week for 40 years and retire, then rest assure you will get exactly that.

Bill Gates wired into his brain a different set of affirmations than the large crowd. He stepped out of the norm and created Microsoft words of affirmation and this stepping out of the norm yielded him a life that stands apart from the normal affirmations of lack. The few people who followed him took on a new mental organization in which they believed enough in his affirmation of abundance in computer programs.

What words have you affirmed in your mind? Have you affirmed problems or have you affirmed abundance? Have you focused more attentions on bills and confrontations or have you focused more on wealth and peace? Where is your point of awareness?

How are you implicitly affirmed to react to challenges in your life situations? Have you mentally prepared yourself to respond to money as of though it is abundant or have you prepared your response to be one of lack and not enough? If you look closely at how you feel and the certain way you act towards money you will see that your world and experiences about money comes to you in an exact proportion of your corresponding inner state.

CONCLUSION

Mental models tend to be functional rather than complete or accurate representations of reality. A mental model is a simplified representation of reality that allows people to interact with the world. Because of cognitive limitations, it is neither possible nor desirable to represent every detail that may be found in reality. Aspects that are represented are influenced by a person's goals and motives for constructing the mental model as well as their background knowledge or existing knowledge structures, which, as noted above, may be conceptualized as 'mental models existing in long term memory'. Mental models thus play a role in filtering incoming information. The theory of 'confirmation bias' (Klayman and Ha 1989) suggests that people seek information that fits their current understanding of the world. Incoming information may reinforce existing mental models or may be rejected outright.

Different fields of study are interested in, and therefore view, the inaccurate and incomplete quality of mental models differently. Those applying the mental model construct to complex systems regard the mapping process involved in constructing a mental model as a many-to-one 'homo-morphic' mapping. This involves decomposing a complex system into a number of smaller models representing subcomponents of the system. Conceiving the construction of mental models in this way suggests that the model is an "imperfect representation" and acknowledges that people make errors (Moray 2004). Similarly, systems dynamics researchers draw attention to peoples' cognitive limitations in terms of processing information feedback, particularly when there are long time delays between action and response (Sterman 1994). Controlled experiments, mainly computer-based, show that people's mental models demonstrate a limited capacity to take account of feedback delays and the side effects of decisions made (Doerner 1980, Brehmer 1992). In his study of mental models, Sterman (1994:305) concluded that "people generally adopt an event-based, open-loop view of causality, ignore feedback processes, fail to appreciate time delays between action and response and in the reporting of information, and are insensitive to non-linearities that may alter the strengths of different feedback loops as a system evolves". This literature treats these limitations in people's mental models as presenting an impediment to learning; it assumes that addressing the limitations and critical flaws in mental models can improve system functionality.

Despite their potential limitations, individuals' mental models are not necessarily amenable to alteration. As the psychology literature recognizes, people tend to filter new information according to its congruence or otherwise with their existing understandings, beliefs, and values. They may reject discrepant evidence, or compartmentalize it within a subsystem of larger systems of understanding.

www.ingramcontent.com/pod-product-compliance
Lightning Source LLC
Chambersburg PA
CBHW060415290526
45791CB00002B/768